THE IIA RESEARCH FOUNDATION

For more than 25 years, The Institute of Internal Auditors has looked to The Research Foundation to define leading internal audit practices and to promote the profession to academic institutions. The Foundation's board of trustees recently redefined their mission as:

"To be the recognized leader in sponsoring and disseminating research, to assist and guide internal auditing professionals and others, in the areas of risk management, controls governance processes and audit practices."

The Research Foundation is committed to:

- Defining internal auditing practices as performed by global leaders in research reports.
- Educating practitioners, educators, and the general public about the merits of internal auditing.
- Distributing materials on the benefits of internal auditing to organizational leaders and clients.

To continue to benefit from this ongoing effort and to help The Foundation fund top-quality research studies and educational programs for internal auditors worldwide, join the Master Key Program. For $1,000, your organization can become a subscriber and receive all Research Foundation publications and research reports as soon as they come off the press.

Master Key subscribers will receive reports on topics like:

- *Corporate Governance*
- *Privacy*
- *Continuous Monitoring*
- *Electronic Commerce*
- *Internal Auditing Practices*

To subscribe to the Master Key Program, call +1-407-937-1356 or e-mail: research@theiia.org

---

Count on The IIA Research Foundation to help you perfect your profession and empower your success. Subscribe today.

To order individual copies of Research Foundation reports:
Online: www.theiia.org under The IIA
E-mail: iiapubs@pbd.org

PC MANAGEMENT BEST PRACTICES: A STUDY OF THE TOTAL COST OF OWNERSHIP, RISK, SECURITY, AND AUDIT

By
Mark Salamasick, CIA, CISA, CSP
Charles Le Grand, CIA, CISA, CDP

With Cooperation and Assistance From:
the American Accounting Association (AAA),
the American Institute of Certified Public Accountants (AICPA),
the Information Systems Security Association (ISSA),
and the National Association of Corporate Directors (NACD)

This report conforms to the COSO framework, is consistent with ISO 17799, and augments the *Systems Assurance and Control (SAC)* framework.

The Institute of Internal Auditors Research Foundation

Disclosure

The IIA RF publishes this document for informational and educational purposes. This document is intended to provide information, but is not a substitute for legal or accounting advice. The IIA does not provide such advice and makes no warranty as to any legal or accounting results through its publication of this document. When legal or accounting issues arise, professional assistance should be sought and retained.

The Professional Practices Framework for Internal Auditing (PPF) was designed by The IIA Board of Directors' Guidance Task Force to appropriately organize the full range of existing and developing practice guidance for the profession. Based on the definition of internal auditing, the PPF comprises *Ethics* and *Standards, Practice Advisories,* and *Development and Practice Aids,* and paves the way to world-class internal auditing.

This guidance fits into the Framework under the heading *Development and Practice Aids*.

ISBN 0-89413-528-7
03562 11/03
First Printing

CONTENTS

ABOUT THE AUTHORS

Mark Salamasick CIA, CISA, CSP
Mark.Salamasick@utdallas.edu
Director of Endorsed Internal Audit Program, University of Texas at Dallas

Mark Salamasick served as the Research Project Leader for The IIA Research Foundation on this project. He is director of a newly created IIA Endorsed Internal Audit Program at the University of Texas at Dallas. The program has a significant emphasis on technology, information security, and business process design. He teaches "Information Technology Risk Management," "Business Process Design and Internal Audit," and "Financial Statement Analysis" at the University. He also is a principal with Coordinated Risk Management and Audit, which performs independent audit and risk management services.

Mark was previously with Bank of America for over 20 years where he worked until the end of 2002. During his last two years at the bank he was in a role of Senior Vice President of Internet/Intranet Services. The group was responsible for all Web-hosting services and infrastructure for the bank. In that capacity he was responsible for establishing and chairing the process for all e-business architecture standards and products. Prior to that he served in the role of Senior Vice President and Director of Information Technology Audit at Bank of America. He worked within the Internal Audit Group of the bank for 18 years and gained experience in technology, financial, and operational auditing. He had responsibility for partnering and auditing technology, information security, and business continuity during those years. Prior to joining Bank of America, he was a senior consultant at Accenture (Andersen Consulting).

Mark has worked in various capacities with The IIA, including the last three projects related to *Systems Auditability and Control (SAC)* in 1990, 1993, and 2001. He recently completed a Handbook for The IIA, *Auditing Vendor Relationships*. He is published in the areas of internal audit, information security, and business continuity.

Charles Le Grand, CIA, CISA, CDP
clegrand@theiia.org
Assistant Vice President, Technology Practices, The Institute of Internal Auditors

Charles Le Grand is Assistant Vice President of Technology Practices for The Institute of Internal Auditors (IIA). He provides direction to all areas of The IIA in the use of technology to deliver programs and products for the internal auditing profession, and addresses current and emerging issues in technology that impact the profession. This includes research and educational programs to study and promote progress of the profession and individual internal auditors. He was Director of Research for The IIA Research Foundation before accepting his present position.

Le Grand is staff liaison to The IIA's International Advanced Technology Committee. He serves on the Board of Directors of the Partnership for Critical Infrastructure Security, on the Advisory Board of the Center for Continuous Auditing, and interfaces with other organizations concerned with technology and its security, control, auditing, and educational aspects. He also was IIA's staff member responsible for the landmark *Systems Auditability and Control (SAC)* research projects in 1990 and 1993, and the Information Security Management and Assurance report series and audit summits in 2000 and 2001. He also introduced IIA's first two Web sites: www.TheIIA.org, and www.ITAudit.org.

ACKNOWLEDGMENTS

The Institute of Internal Auditors Research Foundation (IIARF) acknowledges and greatly appreciates the sponsorship, participation, assistance, and general cooperation of Intel Corporation in support of this project. Without their assistance this project would not have been possible.

The IIA relies on its members worldwide to support progress of the profession of internal auditing. IIA's motto is "Progress Through Sharing," and this project exemplifies that motto. This document and the research that went into its development came into being only by the generous support of the many individuals and organizations who shared their time and expertise through the survey process, forum presentations, case studies, and numerous discussions about current and emerging issues and best practices.

The authors specifically express appreciation to Ray Kollar, Rob Shiveley, and Kim Marion of Intel for their support and for providing guidance from the beginning through the end of the project. Thanks are also due to many members of The IIA headquarters staff for their personal efforts in support of the Technology Audit Forum. We particularly thank Susan Lione, CIA, Jodi Swauger, CIA, Louise Whitsett, Nicki Creatore, and Basil Pflumm, CIA, for their assistance throughout the project. We also express our thanks to Donald Sparks, CIA, from The IIA's online services group for his timely assistance on the survey as supported by the same process and technology that provide the Global Auditing Information Network (GAIN) benchmarking and flash survey services.

The Technology Audit Forum for this project was made possible by subject matter speakers from many different areas. We wish to thank each of the forum speakers and their respective companies for their participation in the event. Materials from the speakers have been integrated throughout this report, and we are grateful to each of them for the significant amount of time they spent covering the key issues of our research focus.

Peter Kastner, Aberdeen Group, served as the keynote speaker to kick off the event and helped focus on the technology areas confronting us today. Mark Salamasick briefed the group on the current status of the survey and best practices. Tim Burke, Aon Financial Services Group, and Kurtis Suhs, NetDiligence, addressed current practices regarding network insurance, which has experienced significant change in recent years. Jeff Curtis, Ernst & Young, addressed the group regarding return on security investment using information from a research study performed through the Ernst & Young Business and Economics Analytics Group.

Jay Stott, Fidelity Investments, covered the role of internal audit in addressing emerging PC technology. Peter Kastner facilitated a panel on the total cost of ownership of the enterprise PC with Suzanne Hopgood, Hopgood Group, Mark Lutchen, PricewaterhouseCoopers, Thomas Pisello, Alinean, and Thomas Stewart, Intel. Tripp Davis, PricewaterhouseCoopers, covered the IT implications of regulatory changes, including Sarbanes-Oxley. Susan Watson spoke to the group on information security issues and moderated the concluding session on information security with Jeff Curtis, Kim Walker, JP Morgan Chase, Tripp Davis, and Steve Skibinski, Intel.

We particularly thank Susan Watson, who served as the moderator during the day-and-a-half session and offered her knowledge and experience to the forum content. Special thanks are also due to Suzanne Hopgood who, representing the National Association of Corporate Directors (NACD), provided the board and audit committee perspectives to the forum proceedings and went the extra mile to present key issues as our after-dinner speaker.

We especially thank Tim Burke, Aon, for his assistance in writing Chapter 2, Business Risk Assessment and Insurance. Tim developed the parts of the chapter that provide new information about changing coverage for networks, and about consulting with companies that review network insurance coverage. Tim was a key participant in the Technology Audit Forum, and provided additional time to consult with the researcher during this project on various matters related to network risk insurance. Many other individuals also contributed their time and expert insights to this project. Our thanks go to the Report Review Team, The IIA's International Advanced Technology Committee, and to The IIA Research Foundation's Board of Trustees and Board of Research Advisors who provided support and assistance.

All of the following organizations were represented as part of the review team and were part of the team endorsing the final report: the American Accounting Association (AAA), the American Institute of Certified Public Accountants (AICPA), the Information Systems Security Association (ISSA), and the National Association of Corporate Directors (NACD).

Much of the guidance and structure for this project was based on the Committee of Sponsoring Organizations of the Treadway Commission (COSO's) *Internal Control - Integrated Framework,* which was also used in planning the project survey. We also considered the new guidance provided in COSO's *Enterprise Risk Management Framework* that was circulated as an exposure draft at the time of this writing. This project followed many of the principles previously established throughout earlier *Systems Assurance and Control (SAC)* projects. We specifically thank Fred Palmer for his long-standing support for the *SAC* projects, and for the insights and guidance he provided as we developed our research approach and documented our results in this report.

The forum participants who volunteered to make up the audience added their insights, questions, perspectives, and concerns during the proceeding. Each made an active contribution to the event. We would like to thank Mark Stanley, Carnival Corporation, who recommended the specific title for this research report at the forum proceedings.

The Institute of Internal Auditors Research Foundation

The individuals who gave their personal time and provided professional expertise in reviewing the drafts and final copies of the report added measurably to its content, format, and value. We are grateful to each one. We also note that the identification of the reviewers and their organizations does not necessarily imply an endorsement on the part of those organizations.

Forum Speakers:

William G. Bishop, CIA	The Institute of Internal Auditors
Timothy Burke	Aon
Jeffrey A. Curtis	Ernst & Young
Tripp Davis	PricewaterhouseCoopers
Suzanne Hopgood	Hopgood Group
Peter S. Kastner	Aberdeen Group
Mark Lutchen	PricewaterhouseCoopers
Thomas Pisello	Alinean LLC
Mark L. Salamasick, CIA	University of Texas at Dallas
Steve Skibinski	Intel Corporation
Thomas C. Stewart	Intel Corporation
Jay Stott, CIA	Fidelity Investments
Kurtis E. Suhs	NetDiligence
Kim D. Walker	JP Morgan
Susan Watson	CXO Media Inc.

Forum Participants:

Beth Breier	City of Tallahassee
Elizabeth A. Calamito	Highlands Insurance Group
Ovie Carroll	United States Postal Service
Carl L. Case	Florida Technical College
Vickie L. Caughron, CIA	Oak Ridge Associated Universities
Glen D. Chambers	Government Audit Training Institute
Richard F. Chambers, CIA	The Institute of Internal Auditors
Mark Chiancola	International Steel Group Inc.
Thomas J. Cianflone, CFSA	Lee County Clerk of Circuit Court
Jacqueline Couch, CIA	St. Petersburg, City of
Lori K.M. Cox, CIA, CGAP	Pascua Yaqui Tribe
Robert R. Darby	Dallas/Ft. Worth International Airport
Cory Douglas Domayer	Halifax Community Health System
Somaia Farag, CIA, CGAP	Governors Office
Terri Freeman, CIA	Publix Super Markets Inc.
David A. Furst	Air Force Audit Agency
Timothy J. Galvin, CFSA	

Allan Geetter	University of Hartford
Kenneth M. Gentile, CCSA	Associated Marine Institutes
Rob Gentile	Christiana Care Health System
Karin M. Grant	Lee County Electric Cooperative, Inc.
John W. Griffith, CIA	Progress Energy Service Co.
Glenn C. Harmon	Harris Corporation
Karl H. Heins	University of California
Kevin Hickey	LandAmerica Financial Group Inc.
Alan G. Itzkowitz	University of Hartford
Stephanie Keeney	Bank of America
Jayawant Govind Khandeker	Walter Industries Inc.
Donald R. Kimmel	AAA
Karl S. Kispert	
Ray Kollar	Intel Americas, Inc.
Sarah Kosberg	Florida Department of Transportation
Linda R. LaMarr, CIA	Richmond City Board of Education
William Landshof	Trustmark Insurance Company
Kenneth H. Laraway	WS Badcock Corporation
Charles H. Le Grand, CIA	The Institute of Internal Auditors
John J. Leeson	National Center for Forensic Science
Cynthia LeRouge	University of Southern Florida
Rosalyn G. Mansour	
Tim McCollum	The Institute of Internal Auditors
Mary L. McGauley	First National Bank of Central Florida
Ronald Merryman	U.S. Postal Service, IG
Thomas A. Mock, CIA	Hughes Supply Inc.
Donald J. Nelson, CIA	Nelson Associates
Sam Onwuanaibe	Harris Corporation
David T. Orszulak	Professional Resources International
Jon Pattelli	Argonne National Laboratory
Basil H. Pflumm, CIA	The Institute of Internal Auditors, Inc.
Frank V. Phillips	Diebold Inc.
Richard Pope	Cerebit
Steven Proctor	Intel Corporation
David E. Richstone, CIA	North Broward Hospital District
Randall Riley	American Automobile Association (AAA)
Gary Rippie	United States Postal Service OIG
Michael Roberti	Harris Corporation
Robert M. Ruhge	Harris Corporation
Wesley C. Sampson	

Michael E. Seagraves	City of Tallahassee
Robert Shiveley	Intel Corporation
Mark Stanley	Carnival Cruise Lines Inc.
Larry Stewart	The Institute of Internal Auditors
Dan M. Swanson	The Institute of Internal Auditors
James Jeffrey Swauger	National Center Forensic Science
Johanna S. Swauger, CIA	The Institute of Internal Auditors
Marcia L. Weidenmier	Texas Christian University
Dennis R. Wiggins	Halifax Community Health
David R. Williams	Southwest Airlines
Henry Major Winter, CIA	W.S. Badcock Corporation
William J. Wyatt	TECO Energy Inc.

Report Reviewers:

Peter Allor	Internet Security Systems
Alexandre Apparecido	Brasil Telecom
Ken D. Askelson, CIA	JCPenney Company, Inc.
Stewart Baker	Steptoe & Johnson, LLP
Mary Bieker	Marsh USA Inc.
Alexandra Branisteanu	SAIC IT Systems
Stephanie Bryant	University of South Florida, and American Accounting Association
Timothy Burke	Aon
Dave Cullinane	Washington Mutual, Inc., and Information Systems Security Association
Jeffrey A. Curtis	Ernst & Young LLP
Christine Di Fabio	Financial Executives International
Russ Gates	Dupage Consulting LLC
Howard Glavin	Internet Security Systems
Peter Gleason	National Association of Corporate Directors
Douglas Guerrero	EDS
Mary Guzman	Marsh USA, Inc.
Eric Hespenheide	Deloitte & Touche
Michael Hines, CIA	Purdue University
Mark Hornung	Ernst & Young LLP
Christopher Keegan	Marsh USA, Inc.
Alexandra Lajoux	National Association of Corporate Directors
Cindy LeRouge	St. Louis University
Chris Linsteadt	Coordinated Risk Management and Audit Services

David Lione	KPMG LLP
Mark Lutchen	PricewaterhouseCoopers
Narender Mangalam	AIG eBusiness Risk Solutions
Louis Matherne	AICPA
Steve Mezzio	Resource Connection
John Mills	University of Nevada
Alan Oliphant, MIIA	Mair International
Will Ozier	OPA Inc., The Integrated Risk Management Group
Ed Pitkin	Business Writing for Web and Print
Michael Rasmussen	Giga Information Group, and Information Systems Security Association
Kurt Reding	Pittsburg State University
Larry Rittenberg, CIA	University of Wisconsin
Seth Shapiro	Marsh USA, Inc.
Maury Shenk	Steptoe & Johnson. LLP
Kyoko Shimizu	Shin Nihon & Co., and IIA Japan
Brian Spindel	SecurePipe Incorporated
Jay H. Stott, CIA	Fidelity Investments
Dan M. Swanson	The Institute of Internal Auditors
Jodi Swauger, CIA	The Institute of Internal Auditors
Marcia Weidenmier	Texas Christian University
Karen Woo	Consultant, and American Bar Association, Information Security Committee
Lee Zeichner	LegalNet Works, Inc.

CHAPTER 1
EXECUTIVE SUMMARY

Introduction

This report provides guidance to corporate directors, managers, auditors, and other advisors for addressing the business and technical controls related to personal computers (PCs), and for understanding the overall impact of the PC on the business control environment. By gaining a basic understanding of the key elements of PC management:

- Directors can exercise better oversight in this area.
- Managers can exercise stronger leadership.
- Auditors can consult with executive, financial, technology, and operational management on maintaining effective PC and network security.

Management can then assess the true costs of the networked PC environment; managing software and other PC components; and maximizing PC contributions to business efficiency and security.

This report also provides guidance for assessing and documenting PC controls in light of an increasingly stringent regulatory environment that can significantly impact technology implementation in general, and PC management in particular.

Beyond the PC — Managing the Array of New Client Devices
Though desktop and mobile PCs are likely to remain the core personal productivity tool for most workers, a variety of other client devices have entered the mainstream, including personal digital assistants (PDAs), cell phones, and handheld computers. With the rapid emergence of wireless, these and many other devices are becoming, or will soon become, part of the networked environment. Though this report focuses on the PC, most of the principles, strategies, and technologies discussed are applicable to these other devices. By integrating all client devices into the PC management strategy, enterprises can leverage tools and processes to improve value, reduce risk, and better manage total costs.

The Importance of the PC

Amidst the complexity and cost of data centers and core business applications, it is easy to overlook the importance of the ubiquitous and seemingly inexpensive PC. Yet desktops and today's increasingly mobile notebooks are involved in an enormous variety of business processes. A large percentage of employees in most businesses could not fulfill their job function without a working PC. A simple way to gauge its importance is to multiply the number of PCs by the $8,000 to $9,000[1] per year that represents the total cost of ownership (TCO) per system in a typical enterprise environment.

Of course in today's networked world, it is also necessary to consider the risk associated with failed, infected, or hacked PCs, which can result in lost productivity, lost business opportunity, damaged credibility, and extensive liability if third-party data or systems are negatively impacted. In our increasingly security-conscious world, these issues are growing in importance and must be addressed by all responsible organizations.

As will be demonstrated in this report, best practices for PC fleet management can reduce total costs by 20 percent to 25 percent for a typical company — while improving the security, performance, reliability, and agility of the infrastructure and the enterprise. A knowledgeable auditor can play a key role in bringing about these changes.

About this Report

This report is based on research and collaboration with leading experts in the business issues that surround the use and management of networked PCs. There were four major phases of research and preparation:

1. An extensive review of literature and guidance
2. An online survey accomplished via The IIA's Global Auditing Information Network (GAIN) Flash Survey process
3. A Technology Audit Forum that convened leading experts in the field of technology, security, audit, and corporate governance
4. Extensive review and revision of the report by a strong cadre of volunteers and partner organizations

[1]Estimates of total cost of ownership for PCs vary depending on the environment, configurations, elements addressed in TCO calculations, etc. Rather than establishing a recognized annual TCO for PCs, this report presents estimates provided by the various organizations and experts participating in the research project.

To provide an appropriate framework for the issues discussed in this report, survey questions were organized around the Committee of Sponsoring Organizations of the Treadway Commission (COSO's) *Internal Control - Integrated Framework.* Parts of the report are also designed to address the new COSO *Enterprise Risk Management* report exposure draft that was circulated when this report was being prepared.

In presenting the results of these efforts, this report looks at six key issues that are of fundamental importance to most organizations:

1. Business Risk and Insurance
2. Compliance and Regulatory
3. Information Security and Appropriate Use
4. Business Continuity
5. Software Currency and Management
6. Total Cost of Ownership and Finance

The core findings for each of these issues is presented below and discussed in greater detail in the corresponding chapters.

Business Risk and Insurance

The business benefits of global connectivity via the Internet are undeniable — and so are the risks. Internet-connected PCs are subject to frequent attacks from viruses, worms, hackers, and other digital threats, and are also subject to internal misuse from authorized employees. The connection of backend systems to networked PCs adds to the risk with the potential for compromising large quantities of business data or third-party information. No longer can management or other system users afford to be naïve about PC practices as these will not only impact their own organization, but also their business partners, customers, other users of the Internet, and even critical environmental, economic, and defense infrastructures.

Traditional insurance policies were not designed to cover these risks, and most now carry explicit exclusions for network-related security events. Network insurance policies have been established to cover this gap. These policies are typically modular in nature, enabling companies to construct customized coverage based on their specific risk profile. However, coverage is qualified based on the level of internal controls established for the PC environment. In fact, without comprehensive and documented controls, it may be impossible to get coverage at all; or businesses may find that detailed exclusions prevent them from collecting when a crisis strikes.

A risk management program is therefore necessary to quantify "value at risk;" identify vulnerabilities; implement appropriate internal controls based on an organization's risk appetite; and define insurance needs to cover residual risk. The *Systems Assurance and Control (SAC)* model provides an extension of the *Internal Control - Integrated Framework* to address information and security management within the business context. COSO establishes a well-tested, comprehensive framework, while *SAC* integrates essential concepts related to the use and control of information technology.

Comprehensive and documented internal controls lie at the heart of effective PC fleet management. Policies should extend from generalities at the highest organization levels, down to the specific technologies and processes deployed in and around the PC infrastructure. Enterprise standards are essential to limit complexity and support automated tools and efficient processes for strategic planning, asset management, deployments and upgrades, software licensing and maintenance, and core security functions such as firewalls, virus protection, and event logging.

Wireless Value and Business Risk
Wireless mobility is adding to the value of the PC infrastructure — and the importance of effective security and risk management. Access anywhere and any time has become a creed for many businesses, and wireless technology is clearly the next wave of advancement. The value should not be ignored, yet neither should the risks. In the survey results for this project, only 21 percent of respondents had performed a cost analysis for wireless, and only 30 percent addressed wireless as part of the policy/procedures for PCs. Providing a strong system of internal controls to enable rapid but controlled deployment of this new technology should be a priority for many organizations.

See Chapter 2 for more information.

Compliance and Regulatory Issues

In a networked business environment, PC management requirements will be impacted by virtually all legislation and regulation that addresses the integrity, reliability, or privacy of business information. Examples include the Sarbanes-Oxley Act, the International Financial Reporting Standards (IFRS), Basel II, the Corporate Law Economic Reform Program (CLERP), the Gramm-Leach-Bliley Act, the Health Insurance Portability & Accountability Act (HIPAA), and California Law SB 1386. The focus of these regulations is on privacy, financial responsibility and the reliability of reported information — issues that have become deeply dependent on underlying computing systems. Though it is beyond the scope of this document to discuss these regulations in detail, strong PC controls can be instrumental in simplifying and strengthening compliance across a wide variety of these regulations.

Understanding the regulatory and litigating environment is a fundamental component of business risk assessment and responsible management. However, organizations that focus only on regulatory compliance will miss out on the substantial business value of strong and effective internal controls. In the end, strategies and methods become "best practices" because they make good business sense. In some cases it may take a great deal of information gathering and analysis to justify the costs associated with best practices. Other times it may be sufficient to note certain practices are mandated.

Organizations that are driven by compliance can take advantage of this motivation to look more broadly at their policies and operations. As an organization moves toward a comprehensive system of internal controls based on COSO or a similar framework, the value of best practices becomes more quantifiable. Quantifiable benefits may include substantial competitive advantages, and compliance becomes a relatively simple matter of documenting existing processes.

See Chapter 3 for more information.

Information Security and Appropriate Use

> *"In the modern world, everything that business or government does with their information technology becomes part of the global information infrastructure. We must build infrastructure to a very high standard. Attaching weak components to the infrastructure puts your organization as well as your neighbors at risk. Responsible citizens will contribute only sound components to that cooperative infrastructure.*
>
> *"A sound information security program ensures that an organization can rely on its critical business information. Information security is a fundamental and unavoidable cost of doing business and, when provided in a timely and effective manner, protects the health of the organization. Indeed, information security enables competitive advantage and new business opportunities."*
>
> — *Information Security Management and Assurance: A Call to Action for Corporate Governance,* The Institute of Internal Auditors et al., April 2000

In the survey for this research project, 93 percent of respondents reported their organizations had policies governing information security and acceptable use for their PC infrastructure. However, only 33 percent considered their policies and practices to be tightly controlled. Responses indicated numerous areas where prevailing practice falls far short of effective practice. This indicates a significant opportunity to improve security by improving the monitoring and enforcement of control requirements, and by implementing the effective practices described in this report.

The need for better virus protection management came into sharp focus when the Blaster worm and SoBig virus were launched during the time this report was being prepared. These attacks impacted organizations across virtually all industries and the government sector. In some cases entire networks were shut down and PCs were inoperable. Other digital attacks — such as Nimda, Code Red, and the Slammer virus — have had comparable impacts, each one resulting in billions of dollars in global loss due to downtime and cleanup costs.

As many companies learned during these attacks, just having up-to date virus protection does NOT by itself provide an adequate level of protection. A comprehensive approach to managing infrastructure controls must be in place to protect the business from digital threats of all kinds, including not only viruses and worms, but also hackers and malicious insiders. Internal control and security elements such as firewalls, virus protection, intrusion protection, software maintenance and patching, event logging, encryption, authentication, and end-user awareness programs should be carefully controlled and integrated into a larger security framework.

However, even the best applications of controls cannot totally ensure a virus or other threat will not be brought into the environment via a control weakness in an individual machine or a newly discovered vulnerability. Cyber threats can negatively impact the reliability of information and processing, so the networked PC must be regarded as a significant element in the overall system of internal controls. Moreover, business strategy must anticipate threat scenarios based on experience and emerging patterns and continually enhance protection by deploying automated software updates and other protective measures as well as developing and testing response techniques before an attack is launched.

Ultimately, the ability of an organization to deploy, integrate, and manage an appropriate security framework depends on organizational support and funding. This makes it important to understand security requirements within the larger context of business goals and risk management. Organizations that take the extra steps to quantify the total cost and value of PC security will be able to justify essential enhancements based on the return on security investment (ROSI) for each project. Internal auditors can play a crucial role in this endeavor, and help to bridge the conceptual gap that often exists between business and IT decision makers.

See Chapter 4 for more information.

Business Continuity and the PC

As the foundation for individual productivity — and a key component in many core business processes — the PC infrastructure should be recognized as a crucial element in business continuity programs. In any large enterprise, individual PC failure and restoration occurs on a daily basis. A single failure may have limited impact, or the consequences may be serious. It is therefore important to understand the relative importance of business functions and processes as well as their dependence on individual PCs, and to install tools and processes that establish priorities and enable appropriate recovery times.

Business continuity involves integrating recovery policies with help desk functions, data backup solutions, software restoration, and hardware repair or replacement processes. Automated tools for centralized data backup and software image restoration have become recognized best practices, because they not only accelerate recovery, but can also reduce total costs for IT support. Of course, it is less than optimal to tack advanced recovery tools and methods onto a chaotic and poorly managed PC environment. Practices that lead to a standardized, stable, and reliable PC infrastructure ultimately reduce the cost and complexity of PC recovery, and improve enterprise productivity.

Individual PC recovery is relatively simple. Recovering a network of virus-infected systems is far more complex, and requires effective and coordinated action across the enterprise. It is essential to have comprehensive recovery plans in place, supported by well-trained employees who know what to do and when. The impact of a major digital attack can be substantial, and preventative action is essential. However, since no network is 100 percent safe, efficient and coordinated recovery efforts are equally important.

See Chapter 5 for more information.

Software Management and Currency

The environment in which the PC operates is dynamic and will continue to be characterized by significant change and growth. Innovation, spurred by competition and demand, continuously improves hardware and software functionality, performance, usability, and security. Every organization must manage its processes to continually support ongoing changes, updates, and the introduction of new hardware and software. Few, if any, are in a position to scrap their existing technologies and start over from scratch, so diversity of systems adds to the challenges surrounding PC maintenance.

One of the most important software currency issues is security patch management. There is an intense focus on security today, and an active hacker community is ready to capitalize on detected vulnerabilities. The result is an endless series of security patches from leading software vendors. These patches must be evaluated, tested, and deployed to appropriate systems based on a clear understanding of costs and associated risks. This is a significant challenge, yet one which no responsible management team can ignore.

In managing change, businesses must be aware of the risks associated with older PC systems. Software vendors do not provide patches for unsupported systems, but hackers continue to discover vulnerabilities and launch attacks against them. As noted by Aberdeen Group's Peter Kastner, the keynote speaker at The IIA's July 2003 Technology Audit Forum, there are more than 40 million desktop computers running outdated operating systems. Microsoft no longer supports Windows 95, and in 2003 will stop supporting Windows 98 and NT 4.0. Organizations running those older operating systems will no longer receive services such as software bug fixes, security patches, or new software versions. According to Kastner and other industry analysts, this will make these systems difficult or impossible to secure.

Interoperability also plays a major role in managing change. Even though a business function may not need the improved performance or functionality of a new operating system or application, an upgrade may be necessary to maintain compatibility with other software components. In most cases, the best answer is to follow industry developments and carefully manage change to provide a steady migration toward new solutions, with minimal disruption to business or IT practices.

Enterprise PC standards are an essential component of effective change management. A chaotic environment with hundreds of different hardware and software configurations is difficult to manage, and nearly impossible to transition in a cost-effective manner. Of course, standards alone are not a solution. Adopted standards must be appropriate to the organization's environment, technology posture, and culture; and effective mechanisms must be in place to ensure and monitor compliance. Successful solutions are those that automate the management and compliance processes rather than relying on human intervention.

See Chapter 6 for more information.

Total Cost of Ownership and Finance

Auditors traditionally have not dealt with the total cost of ownership (TCO) issue, but now recognize it as an opportunity to add substantial value to the organization. It is equally important to understand the close connection between business processes and the underlying technology infrastructure.

This can enable auditors to quantify the value of specific IT investments and optimizations, so costs can be effectively balanced against risks and benefits.

The good news is that comprehensive best practices for PC management are a win-win opportunity. They not only mitigate enterprise risk and improve productivity, but also can substantially reduce total costs. There is a strong tendency for businesses — especially under difficult economic conditions — to retain PCs as long as they serve their main function. After all, it is hard to argue with the immediate cost savings of delayed acquisition. Yet, as already mentioned, 70 percent to 80 percent of the total cost of PC operation is unrelated to acquisition and deployment costs, and older PCs are inherently more costly to manage and secure.

Here again, there is no one-size-fits-all solution, but a three-year upgrade cycle for desktops and a two-year cycle for laptops seem to deliver best overall value for most organizations, especially when instituted as part of a comprehensive best practices program that includes standardized hardware and software configurations and automated tools for core management functions. Elements to consider when deciding the upgrade cycle should include labor costs, environmental issues, security concerns, tax advantage, and other tangible elements.

Enterprise standards are fundamental to simplifying the PC environment and reducing total costs, yet it is usually not possible to maintain just one standard PC version, or image. Instead, each organization must balance the number of configurations against productivity requirements and optimal refresh cycles. This is usually accomplished with a phased approach — replacing machines and software in groups on a planned schedule. This group approach to upgrades helps ensure a high degree of uniformity, and can be one of the most important factors in controlling TCO.

The research for this report indicates the majority of companies have not yet implemented these best practices. Due to cost pressures, many tend to look at the short term and do not have regular refresh cycles for systems and software. More than 50 percent replace PCs "as needed" or on a cycle greater than four years, 32 percent replace operating systems "as needed," and 54 percent do not have criteria established for operating system upgrades. There is clearly an opportunity for businesses to join the leaders in this endeavor. With careful planning and migration, best practices can deliver a reasonable return on investment during implementation, and lasting value once deployed.

See Chapter 7 for more information.

The Business Case for Sound PC Practices

What is a "best practice?" It is not necessarily what the majority of organizations are doing, but rather a set of integrated processes that have been carefully designed and undertaken in the light of quality management, legal compliance, and efficiency. Best practices become best practices because they deliver, on average, the best total business value in comparison with implementation costs. Perhaps most importantly, best practices incorporate internal controls that allow businesses to quantify the value of the practices themselves, and move toward customized operational practices that deliver increasing value.

As discussed throughout this report, best practices for PC management impact an enormous variety of key business issues, from risk management and insurance, to legal and regulatory compliance, to business agility, to enterprise productivity, and the total cost of ownership. The PC has been around for many years, and its impacts are pervasive and increasing. Though the e-business hype has gone the way of the dot-com boom, the movement toward Internet-based solutions continues, with associated improvements in workflow efficiency and cost reduction — and increased dependency on the reliability and security of the PC infrastructure. With these developments, PC management is no longer an administrative function with limited impact on the organization. The PC infrastructure has become a strategic business asset, and should be managed accordingly.

Enterprise Call to Action

As stated in *Internal Control - Integrated Framework*, the "Tone at the Top" sets the control environment for an organization. A move toward PC management best practices is a complex undertaking. It requires a considerable investment and a commitment from the highest levels of the organization. However, as is indicated throughout this report, a comprehensive program is increasingly essential to manage risk — and can deliver bottom-line value to the business through lower total costs and higher productivity.

This report can be used to initiate and support discussions between finance, technology, audit, and executive management toward identifying and benchmarking areas where your enterprise has room for improvement. As was repeatedly demonstrated during this research, "there is no single silver bullet." This became even more evident during the writing of this report, as we found it difficult to logically isolate one chapter from another. With careful implementation, improvements in a single area can ripple throughout the PC environment, and the impact of multiple improvements will be greater than the sum of the parts.

There is nothing simple about PC management best practices, but our number one recommendation *is* simple: begin now. Ultimately you will need to consult many sources to establish optimized practices (see Appendix C). This guide can provide a framework for that effort. It can also help to initiate your pursuit toward more reliable operational and information controls, better regulatory compliance, reduced TCO, and the optimization of technology for continuous improvement of your business practices. Start the process with a Management Assessment and Internal Audit Review (see Appendix G).

CHAPTER 2
BUSINESS RISK ASSESSMENT AND INSURANCE

Introduction

Effective controls at the PC level are an essential component of overall business management. In fact, the lack of sufficient controls has been the cause of total network outages for many organizations, with associated lost business opportunities. A high-quality solution will incorporate many of the best practices discussed throughout this report. However, every organization will have its own business risk strategy and will therefore adapt these best practices as needed and structure its system of internal controls accordingly.

The risk model for establishing PC controls should be comprehensive enough to account for the broad impact of the PC on business processes. Enterprise security, productivity, infrastructure agility, the total cost of ownership, regulatory compliance, and legal liability should all be addressed. Since there is no such thing as a completely secure PC or network, insurance will continue to play a key role by transferring residual risk once appropriate internal controls have been established. Security and related insurance is an area that has undergone — and continues to undergo — much change. Threats and vulnerabilities are constantly evolving, which alters the type and amount of coverage needed. Insurance providers are also modifying their policy provisions to ensure they do not cover more risk than they are willing to accept.

To manage risk in this volatile environment, organizations should closely assess their current coverage to be sure it fits their risk profile and business requirements. They should also be aware that internal controls can have a significant impact on insurance rates, including the ability to obtain coverage at all. The stakes are high, and IT organizations should have formal processes in place to regularly monitor, evaluate, and enforce internal controls to ensure compliance with internal objectives, legislation, regulations, agreements, and insurance coverage provisions.

Risk Model

The business risk model must be closely tailored to match each organization's dynamic internal and external environment, including its unique mission, strategies and objectives, and the market forces and other factors that impact its success. Control structures for operations, reporting, compliance, and safeguarding should be designed to move the organization toward its desired results, reduce inherent risk, and manage residual risk. Of course, these factors depend on each organization's risk appetite, which will vary with the regulatory environment in their particular industry, and with stakeholder expectations and the importance of protecting results and reputation.

Many organizations use COSO's *Internal Control - Integrated Framework* as a control model. COSO is generally regarded as an appropriate model for documenting the reliability of internal controls for compliance with the Sarbanes-Oxley Act. However, although it addresses business control activities, COSO has little to say about the details of supporting technologies. Based on the information gathered during this study, we provide a basic structure for extending the COSO framework to include the key parameters that are essential to effective PC controls (Figure 2.1). This diagram lists the key, high-level issues that should be addressed for each of the five control elements of the COSO framework: Monitoring, Information and Communication, Control Activities, Risk Assessment, and Control Environment. Most of these issues are described in considerable detail throughout this report.

Figure 2.1
COSO Model for PC Management

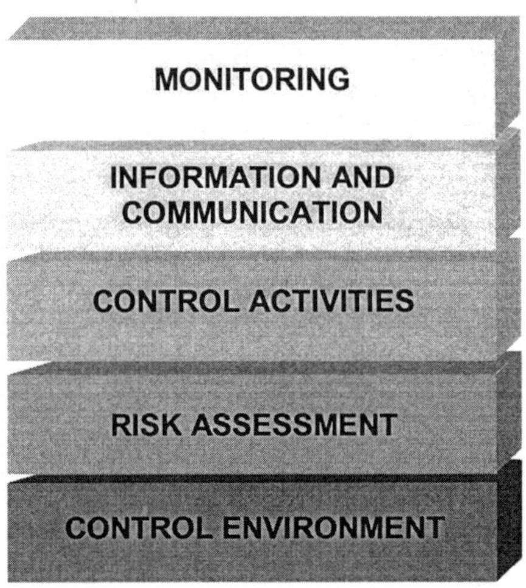

Monitoring:
- Monthly Metrics from PC Help Desk
- TCO Performance Analysis
- Periodic PC Management Assessments
- Internal Audit of Enterprise Networked PC Environment
- Internal Audit of High-risk Areas

Information & Communication:
- Periodic Corporate Communications (Intranet, e-mail, meetings, mailings)
- Call Center Ongoing User Awareness of Best Practices
- PC User Survey
- PC Training
- Help Desk Ongoing Issue Resolution

Control Activities:
- Automated/Frequent Virus Updates
- Automated/Frequent Software Patch Updates
- Automated System and Data Backups
- PC Upgrades and Migration
- Evaluation of TCO Components
- PC Security and Encryption Practices
- PC Standards Compliance Enforcement

Risk Assessment:
- PCs Included in Overall Corporate Risk Assessment
- Individual PC Survey and Risk Assessment
- Differentiate Controls for High-risk PC Areas
- Internal Audit Assessment
- Insurance Assessment

Control Environment:
- Tone from the Top - PC and Security Controls Considered Important
- Corporate Policies - Corporate PC and Security Policy in Place
- Corporate View - Control Over Enterprise Network
- Evaluation of Wireless as an Alternative for Mobility

A highly useful and complementary approach is provided by the *Systems Assurance and Control (SAC) Model*, which expands the COSO framework to include the automated support of business controls, as well as controls for individual technology components and processes. The *SAC Model* is not a direct mapping to PC control issues, but rather provides a framework that is appropriate for all technology-related issues.

Jay Stott, Vice President of Information Technology Audit at Fidelity Investments, is the principal author of the *SAC Model*. He delivered a presentation at the Technology Audit Forum for this research project in which he addressed factors related to planning and managing the PC fleet. He described how PC-related risks are influenced by a variety of factors, including a highly dynamic environment, difficulty in determining total cost of ownership (TCO), and the fact that PCs are typically managed as personal systems and not as enterprise assets. Stott emphasized that a significant part of the problem stems from the fact that PC acquisition costs are generally low, but are only a fraction of TCO. This has resulted in widespread deployment of PCs, typically with inadequate attention to risks, costs, or internal controls. A comprehensive understanding of the total costs and risks associated with the PC infrastructure is essential to drive organizations toward the kinds of formal strategies, policies, and best practices that are appropriate for such a large and distributed enterprise asset.

The *SAC Model* focuses on the key concepts of *availability, capability, functionality, protectability,* and *accountability,* which are widely recognized as business control attributes that are particularly pertinent to IT. These terms are often referred to as business assurance objectives, since they imply a broader range of issues than are traditionally dealt with in a business control framework. In essence, the *SAC Model* helps to ensure that management provides the appropriate infrastructure, resources, and organizational commitment to meet these business assurance objectives using the basic resources that are available — people, technology, processes, investment, and communication. These concepts are described in detail by the *SAC Model*, which is outlined in Appendix F.

Policies, Standards, and Processes

Effective controls depend on a comprehensive framework of policies, including policy statements, standards, and processes. This framework must address the full range of issues outlined in the risk models described above, and must extend across many different levels — from the broad policies set by executives and the board to the detailed technical implementation of policies, such as those enforced by an organization's firewalls or its authentication and authorization solutions. The following lists the basic issues that should be addressed by enterprise policies, standards, and processes for regulating the PC environment. Most of these items are discussed in more detail later in this report.

Roles and Responsibilities

An organization's people must clearly understand their responsibilities for building, maintaining, monitoring, and using the PC environment. This is critical because indirect costs for PC management are typically one of the highest components of TCO. It can be very expensive for users to attempt to learn new software and resolve problems on their own. It is not uncommon for a small department to have an unofficial "PC guru" who spends considerable time and effort supporting other people. These ad hoc approaches to PC management contain many hidden costs, and it is important to establish and manage roles and responsibilities effectively.

Planning and Budgeting

PC hardware and software are assets, and replacement cycles must be planned and budgeted accordingly. This includes deciding how many PCs to deploy and when, and tracking both the hardware and software costs of upgrades. Some organizations have thousands or tens of thousands of servers and PCs. The cost of an individual PC is not high. A good business machine currently runs about $700. However, it costs approximately $8,000 to $9,000 per year to support a PC and user over the useful life of the system. These costs require careful scrutiny, planning, and management.

Acquisition, Deployment, and Disposition

Acquisition, deployment, and disposition are three critical aspects of managing and controlling PCs. Policies should clearly assign authority for equipment purchasing, and standards should identify preferred and allowable systems to buy. The connection of devices into the network should also be carefully controlled to prevent unauthorized or insecure access to network resources. Acquisition and deployment policies should be established to identify who gets what kind of equipment, and how to redeploy systems to new users if and when appropriate.

Disposition applies not only to the physical removal of a PC, but also to the removal of sensitive data and software prior to disposal. There was considerable press coverage about data left on machines from failed Internet ventures after the dot-com implosion. People were buying systems over the Internet that were full of unpurged company data. This is a critical issue, and policies should include proper procedures for removing sensitive information whenever a PC is disposed of or redeployed.

The Importance of Disposition Controls
In 2002, an employee in a Canadian company removed a hard drive from a PC. The PC was being removed from the fleet, but its data had not yet been purged. When the company noticed the drive was missing, they began an investigation and notified several companies that had data on the drive. The drive was subsequently recovered from the employee, but not before one company notified its customers that their information was potentially compromised. To avoid such risks, companies must implement strong physical and logical access control throughout the disposal process. Be sure to also consider related media, such as CDs, USB storage, etc.

Physical Security

Equipment theft is common, so standards should specify how PCs are physically secured. Cable locks can be a good investment, even in supposedly secure locations, since it is not uncommon for a thief to tailgate an employee through a door to steal a PC. The loss of equipment can be trivial compared to the value and sensitivity of information that may be lost or disclosed. (Note: Effective use of encryption can help contain the loss to just that of the equipment.)

A standard after-hours walk-around by security personnel to monitor PC security is another useful strategy. Are systems locked down? Are they left logged into the network or applications? Are passwords written on "sticky notes" attached to the monitor? Security staff can take digital photographs and publish them as "bad examples."

Asset Management

Our research indicates many organizations manage their PC assets poorly. Effective asset management begins by knowing who is responsible for each device on the network. Then, as problems arise, there is a responsible party to contact. It is also important to know each system's hardware and software configuration, its physical location, the identity of all authorized users, the details of access management and authorization, and a PC service contact. Much of this information will change over the life of the system, so accurate tracking can be difficult. Nevertheless, it is essential for efficient fleet management, and to enable timely remediation when problems arise.

License Usage

Most organizations have agreements that stipulate software vendor payments based on actual installation and/or usage. They specify whether and how many copies can be made, as well as vendor expectations for how the organization will track and document compliance. Good license management is important to avoid both overpayment and underpayment, which can result in vendor penalties.

Application Support

Application support is expensive, whether it involves end-user help and training or application patching and troubleshooting. Both tasks involve personnel with specialized expertise, and can include some degree of lost end-user productivity. These costs and activities should be closely monitored and managed.

Operating System Build, Maintenance, and Patching

PC operating systems are subject to frequent vendor updates to repair interoperability issues and to "patch" newly discovered security vulnerabilities. With the frequency and extent of harm attributed to cyber incidents from viruses, worms, and hacking, it is surprising how few organizations have active and thorough policies and processes for software patch management. Of the survey respondents, only 58 percent automatically deliver software patches to the PC environment; and 85 percent deliver patches as needed rather than on a fixed schedule.

Patch management is required for PCs as well as servers. The process is complex and requires a strong and active program that identifies needed patches (not all are critical), distributes them, and audits the environment on a regular basis to be sure they are properly installed.

See Chapter 7 for more information.

Logging

Event logging is supported in today's PC operating systems and should be enabled at an appropriate level on all systems to establish effective audit trails. However, logging must be carefully tuned to avoid excessive information gathering that could conceivably fill up an entire hard drive with nothing but logged events. It is also advisable to establish automated tools for collecting logged information in a central repository where it can be stored and analyzed. Logs from individual systems are useful, but combined data can be used to detect patterns and trends that impact costs and risks across the infrastructure.

Logical Access

Logical access to systems, applications, and information should be fully defined by policy. In a Microsoft Windows environment, the key issue is "administrator rights;" in a Unix environment, it is "super-user rights." Administrators and super-users can access and change anything on a PC — often over the network. In a well-controlled environment, this will not be a long list of people, and it is imperative to carefully control and track who they are. A common strategy among hackers is to attempt to establish administrative rights on any computer they access, so they can set up accounts and passwords, extend their penetration across the network, and cover their tracks.

Firewalls

Firewalls monitor and filter incoming and outgoing traffic between systems and/or networks, and are an integral component of PC security. Traditionally, firewalls have been used at the network perimeter to control access into the enterprise network. However, increasing numbers of PCs — including notebooks and home computers — are active outside network boundaries, and are not protected by the network firewall. In general, these systems should be protected with software-based firewalls that are designed for PCs. Administering software firewalls on a variety of portable PCs can be challenging, since these applications require frequent updating and patching. They also tend to present users with messages that can be confusing and even intimidating. Firewall policies and standards should therefore be carefully constructed to balance the requirements of security and ease-of-use.[1]

Remote Access

A variety of control techniques can be used to manage remote access to various network resources, and to the network itself. Though this is not traditionally seen as a PC issue, the proliferation of wireless notebooks and other remote access devices is raising new security issues that depend on the device as well as on the user and the network resource. Depending on the sensitivity of the information, a simple user ID and password may be sufficient. When greater security is required, one-time-use passwords can provide a higher level of security, and virtual private networks (VPN) can be used to encrypt data that is exchanged over the Internet or wireless networks. Be aware that VPN security only applies to network access and transmitted data. The remote user and machine must also employ appropriate security techniques, or the device or session could be hijacked, which would allow a rogue device to communicate over a trusted connection.

[1]This paragraph is not meant to reflect negatively on firewalls. There are good firewall products available, and some provide centrally managed maintenance to keep them current and simplify the user's role.

Network Segmentation

PC security can be improved by using network switches to segment large networks. This prevents users and devices on one segment from accessing resources on another segment, unless actively configured by an administrator to do so. Typically, servers are not attached to the same network segment as a user desktop, and developers are on yet another segment. (Developers tend to experiment with their systems, and can be a likely gateway for viruses into the network.) Since every PC does not need to talk to every server, this provides a degree of isolation, which can prevent virus proliferation and/or limit impact. In the case of NIMDA, for example, it was discovered that 25 infected PCs could spew out enough e-mail to clog a network of 40,000 connected PCs. However, if those 25 PCs were on a single network segment, only that segment would be impacted. Business could continue as usual on all other segments. It is therefore important to consider PC security issues when establishing policies and standards for network segmentation.

Network Scanning and Host-based Monitoring

PCs can be scanned over the network to determine their hardware and software configuration, including the installation of security patches, firewall updates, and virus signatures. There are also host-based solutions that perform a similar function by installing software agents on each system. These agents then report to a central management application. Either solution can provide an in-depth review of each device on the network to identify vulnerabilities. In many cases both are advisable — a host-based system to control the environment, and network scanning to provide an independent audit of security preparedness.

Cyber Incident Response

Even with the best security controls in place, the issue is not "if" you will be attacked, but rather "when." It is therefore essential to establish policies and procedures that enable a quick and coordinated response to restore functionality. PC cleansing and recovery should be an integral part of that solution. A comprehensive plan should include processes, roles, responsibilities, and sufficient training so people know what to do when a crisis hits.

Encryption

In today's connected organization, data is everywhere, from backend databases, to mobile PCs and PDAs, to CDs, to key chains with flash USB devices. Encryption at the PC level can help to protect that information from theft during both storage and transit. It can protect against the loss of core business assets and the exposure of sensitive third-party information.

However, clear enterprise encryption standards are essential. Without enforced standards, including effective key management, encrypted data can become inaccessible if an employee is unable or unwilling to unlock the data. Consider having a master key somewhere in your encryption scheme so if something happens to an individual, you have the ability to recover their data and protect your company.

Backup and Recovery

For most organizations, the vast majority of data in desktop and laptop computers does not get backed up — at least not on a regular basis. Hard drives do fail and systems can be lost. Appropriate policies, processes, and tools can protect information and reduce employee downtime.

Enterprise Risk Assessment

Our research indicates over 80 percent of organizations include the PC in their overall enterprise risk assessment. Moreover, approximately 50 percent differentiate PC risk based on the applications and business processes performed by the system. For example, if a failed PC is an essential link in an assembly line process, it could cause significant revenue loss unless a rapid response plan or backup machine is in place.

When an individual PC is connected to the enterprise network, it plays a much larger role in enterprise risk considerations, since it can impact other operations through the introduction of worms and viruses or as an access point for hacking from inside or outside the organization. These risks must be managed by providing effective controls at each individual PC and integrating them with the larger control framework.

Insurance and Network Risk

Many organizations are under the impression that their traditional insurance policies cover network security and cyber-related risks, but this is rarely the case. Most standard insurance policies specifically exclude network-related incidents. A failure to understand these exclusions could lead to devastating consequences for many businesses, such as loss of revenue and reputation damage — with no insurance coverage.

Many insurers do offer policies directly covering network risks. According to Tim Burke, Senior Consultant, Aon Technology and Professional Risks Group, "Insurance coverage related to the networked PC environment is still evolving and has gone through significant change in the past two years." Aon defines network risk as "the risks associated with electronic processes and interactions arising from any business activity," such as:

- Loss of/Damage to Intangible Assets.
- Loss of Income/Business Interruption.
- Electronic Content Liability.
- Network Errors and Omissions.
- Breach of Security/Privacy/Confidentiality.
- Release of a Virus, Trojan Horse, or Worm.

The control environment at the desktop and throughout the network is key to understanding these risks and evaluating insurance coverage. An insurance claim can be negated by the lack of due diligence in ensuring controls are adequately enforced (see the sidebar, *The Critical Importance of Due Diligence*).

The Critical Importance of Due Diligence
Tim Burke, Senior Consultant, Aon Technology and Professional Risks Group, discussed the case of a retailer who sustained a $10M loss due to a hacking incident involving a former employee. The company had a $25M first-party network risk insurance policy and submitted a claim to the insurer for the loss. The investigator discovered the software license for the targeted application had not been renewed, and the software vendor had not supported the application for 60 days preceding the hacker intrusion. As is typical of network insurance policies, that company's policy contained an exclusion for software issues resulting from "expiration, cancellation, or withdrawal of support…."

This is just one example of an increasingly common loss. Insurance policies should be carefully reviewed, and thorough controls should be in place to ensure due diligence is practiced in addressing their provisions.

First-party Risk

In network insurance policies, first-party risk is comparable to traditional property insurance. It involves the actual interruption of your network and the associated loss of revenue. Part of that loss includes contingent business interruption, which covers your trading partners if they were affected by your downtime and their revenue stream is interrupted. First-party risk may also include extra expenses, when properly quantified, such as the actual time and resources consumed in rebuilding your system. Many carriers do not provide this coverage because they cannot quantify the risk; or they may include $25 million limits to protect against huge losses from aggregated attacks. In reality, however, most larger financial institutions probably need a billion dollars or more in network risk insurance.

First-party risk may also address intangible property, including theft, damage, or cost to restore these assets. Policies may also cover the failure to safeguard electronic representations of proprietary algorithms, trade secrets, and other intellectual property.

Third-party Liability

Third-party liability, when related to information and networks, is also known as cyber-liability, and is an area of potential litigation. It is considered part of network risk because there is a first party aspect to it. If, for example, you are dependent upon an application service provider, the provided applications are part of your network and the inability to access them means downtime for your business. If you are the application service provider, on the other hand, you need to protect yourself against litigation for your failure to perform. Another example is breach of security and confidentiality, such as failure to comply with privacy legislation. You may also need third-party liability insurance in case PCs in your network are hijacked and used to institute denial of service attacks on other organizations.

The following charts, provided by Aon, identify potential gaps in traditional insurance policies that could subject an entity to unexpected losses. They specifically address property, commercial general liability, and crime insurance contracts.

Table 2.1
The Limits of Traditional Insurance with Respect to Property Coverage

Property Coverage

	Traditional Insurance	Network Risk & Liability Insurance
1	Generally requires "physical damage to tangible property" to trigger coverage.	No tangible property damage is required to trigger coverage.
2	Business interruption/extra expense must be the result of a covered direct physical damage loss.	Forms do no require direct physical damage to activate coverage for BI/EE.
3	No specific coverage for damage as a result of a computer virus, or other malicious code.	Many forms provide specific coverage for computer virus and other malware (worm, Trojan, etc.)
4	Limited coverage, if any, afforded for information assets.	Generally, coverage for intangible assets is afforded for loss as a result of malicious code, unauthorized instructions, and related exposures.
5	Contingent business interruption not covered unless specifically endorsed.	Generally, a basic limit is provided for contingent business interruption, which, in many cases, may be increased.
6	No specific coverage for damage done by "hackers." Damage to Web sites is the most easily anticipated, and to date, most frequently reported, property loss exposure.	Damage caused by hackers may be covered by network liability forms for both first- and third-party risks and liabilities.
7	There is a difficulty in valuing non-tangible property losses.	Valuation is specifically addressed and established by policy language in many forms.
8	There are limited coverage perils even if "all risk except for excluded perils" is provided. The breadth of coverage is not sufficient for e-business exposures.	Coverage perils are generally provided in anticipation of e-business exposures, such as programming error damage, unauthorized use, repudiation of access, and the like.
9	No coverage for Web site extortion-type claims.	Web site extortion is covered under several network liability coverage forms.
10	Policy territory relates to actual location of tangible property.	Policy territory is global, worldwide, or "anywhere."

Table 2.2
The Limits of Traditional Insurance
with Respect to Commercial General Liability Coverage

Commercial General Liability

	Traditional Insurance	Network Risk & Liability Insurance
1	Basic scope of coverage is for "bodily injury liability," "property damage liability," and "personal/advertising liability" as defined (rather narrowly) within the form.	The coverage is designed specifically to address the emerging exposures for network-based business activities with related coverage extensions.
2	"Property damage" (liability) defined as "...physical damage to tangible property..."	Explicit coverage for "intangible property/assets."
3	No coverage for liability arising out of the "tying up" of a Web site connection.	"Denial of Service" is explicitly covered under many network risk forms.
4	Although coverage is afforded for "advertising liability," a usual exclusion exists for "...an offense committed by an insured whose business is advertising, broadcasting, publishing, or telecasting..."	Generally, no similar restrictions in many network risk forms; there can be difficulty in determining the meaning of "whose business is."
5	No coverage for liability of an insured for "breach of security," or unintentional release of confidential information.	"Breach of security" and/or "breach of confidentiality" are usually available for coverage.
6	Generally, very little IP coverage. There is usually limited coverage for copyright/trademark infringement, and never coverage for patent infringement.	Coverage readily available for copyright/trademark infringement; generally, special coverage must be arranged for patent and, at times, trade secrets.
7	Policy territory often restricted to the U.S., its territories/possessions and Canada.	Policy territory is global, worldwide, or "anywhere."
8	Bankruptcy is generally excluded.	Generally, no exclusion for bankruptcy.
9	Financial loss liability (to a customer, for example) is usually excluded	The focus of coverage is usually on the financial impact responsibility of the insured to a third party, and arising out of network-based business activities.

Table 2.3
The Limits of Traditional Insurance with Respect to Criminal Liability Coverage

Crime

	Traditional Insurance	Network Risk & Liability Insurance
1	Valuation of covered losses is a problem (for example, employee dishonesty involving theft of customer records).	Valuation problems anticipated in many coverage forms.
2	"Loss of income" exclusion is normal.	No "loss of income" exclusion in many coverage forms.
3	Damage to "tangible property" is usually required to trigger coverage.	No "tangible property" damage requirement in coverage forms.
4	Generally, coverage afforded for first-party losses (unless third-party coverage is specifically provided.	Many forms provide both a third-party as well as first-party coverage.
5	Computer fraud: theft is generally the basis of coverage.	Much broader approach to "computer fraud" issues under most coverage forms.
6	Computer fraud; no coverage for defense expenses.	Expenses can be provided for under most coverage forms.
7	No coverage, generally, for "crisis control."	"Crisis management" coverage may be provided.
8	Policy territory is generally the same as property/general liability.	Policy territory is global, worldwide, or "anywhere."
9	Generally, no coverage for loss of trade secrets/confidential information.	Not excluded, and may be specifically covered.
10	Electronic Data Processing (EDP) Media is usually valued at the cost of blank materials.	Many insurers provided for specific valuation of intellectual property.

Insurance Product Solutions

While it may be possible to enhance the coverage of a traditional policy to address some of the gaps related to network risk, experience suggests this is challenging in today's environment. Alternatives include increasing risk mitigation efforts to reduce residual risk, or pursuing a stand-alone insurance contract that specifically and explicitly addresses network risks and liabilities. The insurance industry has reacted to new and emerging exposures by creating customized policies. These policies are designed in a modular format to address the specific exposures, business models, and priorities of each company.

- **Online Content Module** — Provides liability coverage for:
  Intellectual Property Infringement (Trademark, Copyright, Title)
  Personal Injury (Libel, Slander, Defamation)

- **Professional Liability Module** — Provides errors and omissions coverage for:
  Internet Service Providers
  Application Service Providers
  Network Security Services
  Web Hosting and Design
  Public Key Infrastructure Services
  E-commerce Transaction Services

- **Network Security Liability Module** — Provides liability coverage for:
  Computer Attacks
  Virus Transmissions
  Unauthorized Access to Data
  Denial of Service
  Disclosure of Confidential Information
  Identity Theft

- **Business Interruption and Intangible Property Damage Module** — Provides indemnification for:
  Loss of Income from Computer Attack
  Extended Business Income
  Dependent Business Income
  Damage to Proprietary Information Assets
  Theft of Proprietary Information Assets

Additional Coverage Options:

- **Cyber Extortion** — Coverage for the investigation and settlement of an extortion attempt.
- **Criminal Rewards** — Coverage for rewards for information that lead to the arrest and conviction of individuals performing computer attacks.

- **Crisis Communications** — Coverage for public relations expenses in the event of an attack.
- **Identity Theft** — Coverage for liability for the theft of personal information of employees, clients, or customers.

Insurance companies known to offer this coverage at the time of this publication include:

- AIG
- ACE UK
- Chubb (Financial Institutions)
- CNA
- Hiscox (a London-based insurer)
- Certain underwriters at Lloyds of London
- Arch Capital
- St. Paul (technology industry specific — no stand-alone coverage)
- Zurich

Enterprise Call to Action

Enterprise risk management, as well as the overall risk assessment performed by internal audit, should specifically include risks that arise in the networked PC environment. This includes the obvious security risks associated with viruses, worms, hackers, and unauthorized or malicious system use, but also the business risks associated with the cost, agility, availability, and performance of the PC infrastructure. These risks are all evolving rapidly, as new threats, technologies, and business models emerge. PC controls must evolve in tandem. This requires close collaboration among business leaders, IT decision makers, security experts, and financial analysts. Internal auditors can play an important role in promoting and managing this cooperation.

Enterprise risk in a networked PC environment can be substantial, and the scope and rigor of controls should be proportional to that risk. To be effective, PC controls must be comprehensive and detailed. They should cover not only PC hardware and software configurations, but also the people, processes, and technologies related to PC and network security, use, administration, and maintenance. To be effective, they must span all organizational levels, from the general policies issued by boards, to the details of implementation that depend on individual technicians and PC users.

Since even the best-controlled PC environment is not risk free, insurance should be an integral part of the overall risk management process. It is imperative that management understands actual coverage and exclusions, and the financial impact on a full range of risk scenarios. It is also important to understand the relationships between coverage and controls, since controls can substantially impact the ability to get coverage, the cost of coverage, and the applicability of coverage when a real event occurs. Most importantly, management should understand that traditional insurance policies do not cover network risk, and that network policies are rapidly evolving. Given the frequency and impact of cyber-related outages, it is critical to track these changes and adapt accordingly.

In closing, it should be noted that enterprise risk management, insurance, and PC controls also depend closely on the legal and regulatory environment for a particular organization. These issues are discussed in detail in the next chapter.

CHAPTER 3
LEGISLATION, REGULATION, AND COMPLIANCE

Introduction

Government and nonprofit regulatory bodies worldwide are playing an increasing role in establishing baseline security requirements for business information technology. Even regulations that do not explicitly focus on security may have substantial consequences for IT in general, and PC fleet management in particular. Examples include the International Financial Reporting Standards (IFRS), Basel II Accord, the Corporate Law Economic Reform Program (CLERP), the Gramm-Leach-Bliley Act (GLB), the Sarbanes-Oxley Act, and the Health Insurance Portability & Accountability Act (HIPAA). These and other laws and regulations focus on issues such as privacy, financial responsibility, and the reliability of reported information. All of these issues have become deeply dependent on underlying computing systems, and will therefore have repercussions on the way businesses use and manage their PC infrastructure.

The PC plays a complex role in many core issues, including security, privacy, information and control reliability, risk management, governance, and even critical infrastructure protection and national defense. Within the overall system of business controls, the PC is both a component subject to control and a tool with which many controls are applied and managed. It is a unique device that defies simple classification. A business PC is a(n):

- Physical asset.
- Processing device.
- Repository for software and information assets.
- Means to access information stored on other devices.
- Communication tool.
- Potential liability, as it can harbor both beneficial and detrimental software and data.
- Point of vulnerability, whereby attackers may introduce harm to the network or system.
- Point of entry for gaining access to other systems and network components.
- Access and egress point for sensitive enterprise or private information.
- Invaluable tool supporting enterprise productivity.
- And much more.

In short, the PC infrastructure presents many issues for management to consider with respect to legal and regulatory compliance in particular, and internal controls in general.

This chapter focuses briefly on today's legal and regulatory environment, then moves on to discuss the overriding value of strong internal controls, and the value of the COSO model for establishing those controls. It then describes some of the key issues regarding internal controls for the PC infrastructure.

The Regulatory Environment

> *Good internal control is no longer just a best practice... It's the Law!*
> — PricewaterhouseCoopers

There is a global move toward tighter laws and regulations for internal controls associated with financial reporting. One of the most far-reaching examples is the Sarbanes-Oxley Act (see below), not because it is the most stringent, but because it cuts across vertical industries and impacts any company that is publicly listed in the U.S. Similar legislation is emerging in many jurisdictions throughout the world.

Privacy legislation is also evolving rapidly. In today's networked business environment, backend data systems are often highly consolidated and are accessible by applications that are, in turn, accessible from the Internet. This is a great boon for accelerating transactions and reducing the cost of doing business. However, it also raises significant new security and liability concerns, and tight controls are necessary to protect individuals, organizations, industries, and economies. Ultimately, any company wishing to take part in the global economy and most national economies will have to demonstrate an appropriate level of internal controls.

Both types of legislation — financial reporting and privacy — have implications for the way companies deploy, manage, and monitor their PC infrastructure. The vast majority of business information is collected, accessed, shared, and sometimes stored on networked PCs, and these systems are often distributed across large geographical regions. Even some relatively large companies keep critical financial information on quick books running on networked PCs. Many others maintain financial information on core business systems, but information on these systems is often input, accessed, and sometimes analyzed using networked PCs. The integrity and security of these networked systems — and the communications between them — are fundamental to the integrity and security of the vast majority of critical business information and processes.

It would be impossible to discuss or even reference all the legislation and regulations that impact PC use and management. We therefore focus on just a few with the understanding that they are representative of a growing regulatory framework that is affecting organizations throughout the world.

The Sarbanes-Oxley Act

> *"The Fortune 1000 will spend $2.5B in initial Sarbanes-Oxley Act (SOA) compliance work, including hefty IT investments, as 85% of companies prepare to make systems changes to support SOA requirements."*
>
> — *Prioritizing IT Investments for Sarbanes-Oxley Compliance,* Lindsey Sodano and John Hagerty, AMR Research, June 2003

Sarbanes-Oxley Act Section 302 requires chief executive officers and chief financial officers of all publicly traded companies in the U.S. to personally certify in each financial report that it does not contain any untrue statements or omit any facts that are material to a true representation of the company's financial condition. They must also acknowledge personal responsibility for establishing and maintaining disclosure controls and procedures, and for disclosing to their auditors and audit committee all significant deficiencies in internal controls that could adversely affect their ability to record, process, summarize, and report financial data. Finally, they must disclose any fraud that involves management or other employees who have a significant role in their internal controls.

Section 404 extends these requirements to the annual reports of these companies. Each report must formally acknowledge the responsibility of management for establishing and maintaining adequate procedures and internal control structures for financial reporting; and provide a full report and assessment of those structures, as of the end of the most recent fiscal year. The organization's public accounting firm must also attest to the accuracy and validity of the assessment. SOA Section 409 makes the need for reporting immediate, and the need for monitoring continuous.

Privacy Legislation

Privacy is well covered in other IIA and IIA Research Foundation reports, and is included here to emphasize the relevance of this issue to PC management. Examples of significant legislation in this area include:

- ***Gramm-Leach-Bliley Act - Financial Privacy*** — The Gramm-Leach-Bliley act requires financial institutions to safeguard customers' records and information against unauthorized access. It applies to "financial institutions" and includes not only banks, securities firms, and insurance companies, but also companies providing many other types of financial products and services to consumers.

- ***HIPAA - The Health Insurance Portability & Accountability Act of 1996*** — It is the responsibility of organizations entrusted with health information to protect that information against deliberate or inadvertent misuse or disclosure. Since much of the relevant data is transmitted through or maintained on PCs, the health-care industry must provide additional measures to ensure patient data is adequately secured.

- ***California Law SB 1386*** — This legislation, which took effect on July 1, 2003, creates new disclosure requirements for any company or government agency that does business with California residents. It requires timely disclosure of any security breaches involving the exposure of unencrypted personal information. It also preserves a private right of action for damages and injunctive relief against any offending company. Because of this, it is quite possible that class action suits could result from noncompliance with this law.

Legal Basis of Liability

In today's evolving regulatory landscape, it is important that organizations understand liability issues with respect to privacy. Many organizations now store and process large volumes of consumer and/or third-party information on internal systems that interact with their networked PCs. Proper management of this information, and the associated systems, depends on the regulatory and legal environment, and on potential liability for compromised information.

The legal firm Steptoe & Johnson LLP covers key liability issues in a recently published paper, "A Patch in Time Saves Nine: Liability Risks for Unpatched Software," by Stewart Baker and Maury Shenk[1]. As the title indicates, their paper focuses primarily on legal liability for security breaches caused by unpatched software, a critical issue for many organizations due to the cost and complexity of effective patch management (*see Chapter 6*). The general conclusions can also be helpful for understanding other liability issues with respect to PC infrastructure management.

In general terms, the Steptoe & Johnson report states that, "Liability for failure to apply security patches could exist either pursuant to statute and regulation, or under common law contract and tort principles." It supports this conclusion by looking closely at some of the key stipulations of the

[1]Stewart Baker is a partner in the Washington, DC, office of Steptoe & Johnson LLP, and heads the firm's Technology Group. Maury Shenk is a partner in the London office of Steptoe & Johnson, and manages the firm's European technology practice.

Health Insurance Portability and Accountability Act ("HIPAA") and the Gramm-Leach-Bliley Act ("GLBA"):

> "Pursuant to GLBA, the four U.S. banking regulators (the Office of the Comptroller of the Currency, the Office of Thrift Supervision, the Board of Governors of the Federal Reserve System, and the Federal Deposit Insurance Corporation) in 2001 adopted interagency guidelines that require any regulated financial institution, among other things, to:
>
> > Protect against any anticipated threats or hazards to the security or integrity of [customer] information; ...
> >
> > Protect against unauthorized access to or use of such information that could result in substantial harm or inconvenience to any customer[; and] ...
> >
> > Design its information security program to control the identified risks, commensurate with the sensitivity or the information as well as the complexity and scope of the bank's activities.[2]
>
> "Likewise, pursuant to HIPAA, the U.S. Department of Health and Human Services in 2003 adopted regulations that require health-care providers, among other things, to:
>
> > Protect against any reasonably anticipated threats or hazards to the security of [health] information[;] ...
> >
> > Implement ... [p]rocedures for guarding against, detecting, and reporting malicious software[; and] ...
> >
> > Implement technical policies and procedures for electronic information systems that maintain electronic protected health information to allow access only to those persons or software programs that have been granted access rights ... .[3]
>
> "These regulatory obligations appear to require the affected entities to implement at least some sort of security patch procedures.
>
> "Both HIPAA and GLBA place responsibility for enforcement of these regulations in the hands of federal regulators, and do not create any right of private individuals to sue based

[2]Interagency Guidelines Establishing Standards for Safeguarding Customer Information, §§ II.B.2, II.B.3, III.C.1, 66 Fed. Reg. 8615 (Feb. 1, 2001).
[3]45 C.F.R. §§ 164.306(a)(2), 164.308(a)(5)(ii)(B), 164.312(a)(1).

> on the regulations (known in legal terms as a "*private right of action*"). However, the regulations provide persuasive evidence of proper security practices, at least in the health-care and banking sectors. Such evidence could be of significant weight in private actions under common law...."

The report goes on to discuss the extent to which GLBA and HIPPA can be seen as representative of trends within the broader regulatory environment:

> "GLBA and HIPPA are not the last security-related initiatives likely to emerge from legislatures and regulatory bodies. Their continued appetite for new rules in the field is demonstrated by the popularity of requiring companies to notify consumers about security breaches. In California, Senate Bill No. 1386 ("SB 1386") took effect in July 2003, requiring any business or other organization to disclose any security breach that compromises unencrypted personal information of California residents (and most large U.S. businesses serve California residents).[4] Significantly, SB 1386 includes a private right of action against organizations that fail to comply with this disclosure obligation. Senator Diane Feinstein of California has proposed federal legislation which would have the same effect on a nationwide basis (without a private right of action),[5] but this legislation so far appears fairly unlikely to make progress in Congress. And in August 2003, the four federal banking regulators exercised their authority under GLBA to issue "guidance" indicating that part of the response by financial institutions to a security breach should be to notify federal regulators, law enforcement and customers.[6] This disclosure guidance as practical matter is binding on U.S. financial institutions. While these disclosure obligations do not directly affect liability for security failures, they will encourage more security-related litigation by telling the victims of security failures exactly who is to blame. In addition, it is only reasonable to expect that lawyers suing over a failure to provide notice of a security breach will also throw in a few counts alleging liability for the underlying breach itself."

The Steptoe & Johnson paper goes on to suggest the SEC could interpret Sarbanes-Oxley Section 404, addressing internal controls over financial reporting, as "extending to controls on computer security, at least for those companies for which a security breach could have a material effect on their business." It also notes similar liability issues are likely to arise under the laws of many countries. The European Union (EU) Data Protection Directive,[7] it notes, "regulates data controllers" that process personal data, and specifically requires implementation of security controls:

---

[4]*See* Cal. Civil Code §§ 1798.29, 1798.82, 1798.84.

[5]S. 1350, 108th Cong. (2003).

[6]Interagency Guidance on Response Programs for Unauthorized Access to Customer Information and Customer Notice, 68 Fed. Reg. 47,954 (Aug. 12, 2003).

[7]Directive 95/46/EC of the European Parliament and Council, Art. 25 (1995).

> Member states shall provide that the controller must implement appropriate technical and organizational measures to protect personal data against accidental or unlawful destruction or accidental loss, alteration, unauthorized disclosure or access, in particular where the processing involves the transmission of data over a network, and against all other unlawful forms of processing. Having regard to the state of the art and the cost of their implementation, such measures shall ensure a level of security appropriate to the risks represented by the processing and the nature of the data to be protected.[8]

Although the directive applies directly only in the EU, it also restricts transfers of data on EU-resident individuals to non-EU countries. The U.S. Department of Commerce and the European Commission in 2000 reached a Safe Harbor Agreement that sets out principles that U.S. companies can agree to follow in order to be permitted to receive data from the EU in compliance with the directive; and many U.S. companies have agreed to follow these principles.[9] One of the Safe Harbor principles, titled "Security," provides:

> "Organizations creating, maintaining, using, or disseminating personal information must take reasonable precautions to protect it from loss, misuse and unauthorized access, disclosure, alteration, and destruction."[10]

> "Other countries have adopted cross-sectoral privacy laws along the lines of the EU Data Protection Directive, such as Canada's Personal Information Protection and Electronic Documents Act ("PIPEDA")."[11]

> "For companies that are subject to the Sarbanes-Oxley Act, the EU Data Protection Directive (including via the Safe Harbor), and similar foreign legislation, these obligations increase the risks associated with unpatched software."

---

[8]Directive 95/46/EC of the European Parliament and of the Council of 24 October 1995 on the protection of individuals with regard to the processing of personal data and on the free movement of such data, Article 17(1).

[9]*See* http://www.export.gov/safeharbor for information on the Safe Harbor Agreement and the companies that have joined it.

[10]U.S. Department of Commerce, Safe Harbor Privacy Principles, available at http://www.export.gov/safeharbor/SHPRINCIPLESFINAL.htm (2000).

[11]S.C. 2000, c.5 (Can.).

The Risk of Liability
In June 2003, the U.S. Federal Trade Commission (FTC) settled a suit against clothing retailer Guess. The suit alleged that Guess had unlawfully failed to protect its customers' privacy because it did not "use reasonable or appropriate measures to prevent consumer information from being accessed at its Web site." In particular, the FTC claimed that Guess had failed to repair Web site vulnerabilities (involving SQL injection attacks — related to the SQL Slammer attack) about which it had known since October 2000, resulting in a successful attack and theft of credit card numbers in February 2002.

The Duty to Patch

How quickly must a software vulnerability be patched? According to Steptoe and Johnson, "In part that will depend on the size of the vulnerability and the urgency of the software producer's recommendation that the patch be installed. But it will also depend on experience; in particular, the speed with which past vulnerabilities have been turned into worms, viruses, or other malware. Here the bar may have been substantially raised by the Blaster worm's two-week turnaround from announcement of the security flaw (and release of the patch) to exploitation. A few more commonly known examples of such rapid exploitation will likely mean that patches must be installed in a matter of days after release to avoid falling foul of the emerging duty of reasonable care.

What if the company is running unsupported or outdated software? In that case, there will be no patch to install. But the lack of a patch will not necessarily excuse the company from liability. The most likely scenario is this: A piece of malware is released that exploits a security flaw that can be found in both a current software product and in that product's no-longer-supported earlier versions. A company using the earlier version falls prey to the malware because no patch has been released. In a lawsuit, the plaintiff whose data was compromised or whose service was interrupted will argue that the company's patch plan should have identified programs that were no longer supported and should have upgraded to a supported version, either as a routine matter or, at least, when a patch was released and the company realized that the only way to install the patch was to upgrade its software. If the court concludes that installation of current security patches is part of the company's duty of care, it almost certainly will not accept as an excuse the fact that the software was so outdated that no patch was available.

Insurance

Also noted from Steptoe & Johnson: "A particularly significant risk from failure to implement security patches relates to insurance. A few years ago, it was difficult to buy affordable insurance for computer security risks. But as the insurance market has begun to understand such risks better,[12] insurance is increasingly available. However, standard insurance policies may not apply where the insured fails to implement available security patches. For example, the AIG netAdvantage Security℠ policy excludes coverage for losses "due to installing or failing to install a software patch."[13] The likelihood or possibility that particular conduct could lead to uninsured liability should have a significant effect on behavior with respect to such potential liability."

Monitoring Risk

The Steptoe & Johnson report offers compelling evidence that a failure to protect customer and third-party information residing on an organization's systems and network will expose that organization to potential litigation and substantial risk. As discussed in that report, the current trend is toward stronger regulations and increasing liability. However, the outcome of current and future litigation will be instrumental in shaping liability with respect to informational privacy. It is important that organizations monitor these developments — along with regulatory changes — to understand their evolving risk environment, and to establish internal controls that are consistent with business need.

The Overriding Value of Internal Controls

Regulatory and legal compliance is clearly an important issue, yet it remains secondary to a larger truth. Regulations typically strive to move businesses toward a baseline implementation of what is commonly accepted as best practices for internal control. As such, the regulatory environment invariably lags behind the implementations of leading companies. Moreover, best practices for internal controls stand on their own merit. They deliver value to the bottom line by improving efficiency and decreasing risk across a wide range of internal and external variables.

Businesses that focus only on regulatory compliance are targeting the lowest common denominator and putting themselves at a competitive disadvantage. On the other hand, companies that focus on best practices for internal controls drive greater value into their business. Regulatory compliance becomes a matter of properly documenting existing controls, rather than implementing major business change.

---

[12] At least the insurance market appears to believe that it understands such risks. Baker and Shenk suggest the increasing likelihood of computer security litigation discussed in this article may have some rude surprises in store for the insurance market.

[13] The fact that the exclusion extends to losses resulting from both installation of and failure to install software patches places insureds in a difficult position, requiring them to install patches, but do so in a fashion that does not disrupt existing operations. Presumably, this requires timely and careful testing of patches in the insured's computing environment.

These advantages are even more compelling in today's dynamic regulatory environment. Strong internal controls position a business to respond more quickly and easily to emerging requirements, whatever they may be. They also help a business to understand and evaluate regulatory requirements within the context of their larger business, financial, and risk environment.

The overriding value of effective internal controls is reflected in the many companies and government agencies that are optimizing their internal control structures, even though they are not regulated by Sarbanes-Oxley. The global competitive and litigative environment is sufficient motivation for most leading organizations to embrace sound business management and control practices and adopt a culture of best practices and continuous improvement. Of course, there are also companies choosing to remain privately held entities specifically to avoid the overhead of Sarbanes-Oxley compliance. Such a strategy is not likely to serve an organization well in the long run.

COSO Control Model

COSO's[14] *Internal Control - Integrated Framework* defines internal control as a process that is effected by an entity's people and designed to provide reasonable assurance regarding the achievement of objectives in: effectiveness and efficiency of operations, reliability of financial reporting, and compliance with applicable laws and regulations.

The COSO framework identifies five interrelated components of internal control:

1. **Control Environment** — People (and their individual attributes, including integrity, ethical values, and competence) and the environment in which they operate.
2. **Risk Assessment** — Awareness of the risks facing the organization; established objectives, integrated with business activities, so the organization operates in concert; and established mechanisms to identify, analyze, and manage related risks.
3. **Control Activities** — Control policies and procedures established and executed to ensure risks are effectively managed and the organization's objectives are achieved.
4. **Information and Communications** — Systems that enable the organization's people to capture and exchange the information needed to conduct, manage, and control its operations.
5. **Monitoring** — Continuous appraisal to allow the control system to react dynamically, changing as conditions warrant.

The COSO internal control components are depicted as a cube (Figure 3.1) relating the internal controls (rows) to the key areas of focus: Operations, Financial Reporting, and Compliance (columns)

[14]COSO – Committee of Sponsoring Organizations of the Treadway Commission. See www.coso.org.

for all the organization's units and activities (third dimension). As the framework indicates, internal control is not a serial process in which each component affects the next, but a multidirectional iterative process in which any component can influence any other.

The iterative nature of controls has long been recognized in IT where the reliability of application or business process controls is dependent on the reliability of controls in the overall IT environment. Business controls over financial information depend in part on IT controls that prevent and detect unauthorized access to financial systems and data. For example, a PC that has been corrupted by a virus or hacker could remain a trusted component of the network with routine access to financial data and systems. This could lead to the disclosure or corruption of financial data, or to the corruption of program code and/or the insertion of rogue programs that could do further damage. Adequate controls at the system and application level are therefore essential to ensure that higher-level business processes are properly controlled. Additional information on COSO is included in Appendix D.

Figure 3.1
COSO Control Model

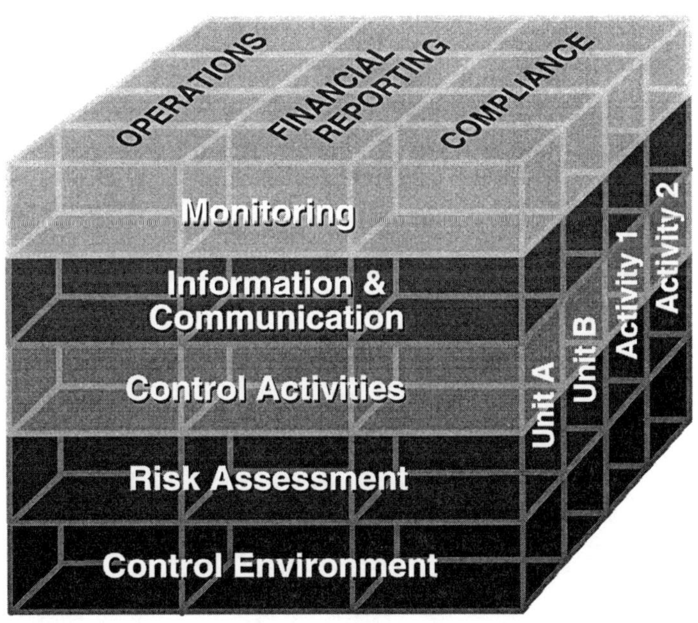

> **Note:** The ISO 17799 standard is another useful framework for technology controls that can be used in support of best practices and regulatory compliance. It focuses primarily on providing a security baseline for evaluating the PC environment.

Maturity of PC Regulatory Practices

In developing an efficient plan for migrating toward optimized internal controls, the concept of maturity can be useful. The maturity of internal controls can be viewed as a progression through five stages:

1. **Unreliable** — The environment is unpredictable and control activities are not implemented.
2. **Informal** — Control activities are in place, but are not adequately documented.
3. **Standardized** — Control activities are in place and documented.
4. **Monitored** — Controls are standardized and periodically tested for effective design and operation.
5. **Optimized** — Controls are fully integrated, monitored in real-time, and continuously improved.

This maturity scale can be useful in evaluating an organization's current internal controls and developing a comprehensive strategy for improving practices and techniques across the organization.

Monitoring and Enforcement of PC Controls

In a well-controlled IT environment, intrusion controls and monitoring should detect unauthorized activity. However, weaknesses in software management and/or monitoring systems could allow such attacks to go undetected. Assuming the attacker gains access to trusted system administration features, he/she may establish accounts and passwords that broaden access and enable the hacker to destroy evidence of unauthorized activity.

The combination of controls needed to prevent and detect such activity includes, but is not limited to, firewalls, intrusion detection, authentication, strong password management, anti-virus measures, restriction of administrator privileges on the PC and network, system change management, monitoring of unusual systems activities, and management review and analysis of financial information and transactions.

The testing and monitoring of activities is critical for effective control. Given the complexity of the environment, automated monitoring is typically required to enable a timely response to any breakdown in control activities. For example, if software patches are not up to date on a networked PC, automated configuration monitoring tools will provide a timely warning for quick remediation.

In the survey conducted for this research, 92 percent of respondents indicated they have controls in place to enforce corporate standards. However, only eight percent of those respondents indicated controls were tightly enforced. When asked about areas where best practices are followed, many cited compliance with software license agreements. No other area specific to regulatory compliance was mentioned.

The Role of the Chief Information Officer (CIO)

The CIO has traditionally maintained custodial responsibility for the organization's financial records and other sensitive business information. The CIO is also typically responsible for custody of the hardware and software resources that process, communicate, and store that information and generate reports.

Typical characteristics and responsibilities of the CIO include:

- Maintaining an effective control environment for the protection of systems, networks, information, communications capabilities, and interfaces with outside parties.
- Organizing and coordinating efforts for technology risk management and compliance with laws, regulations, agreements, policies, and procedures.
- Establishing an appropriate technology risk task force with representation across the enterprise.
- Commissioning or conducting a technology risk assessment and acting on all findings.
- Monitoring the ongoing management of risks related to technology.
- Reviewing new products for security and privacy implications.
- Supporting/delivering employee information security and privacy training.
- Conducting regular security audits, and exposing any internal practices that are not consistent with security policy.
- Monitoring ongoing technology threats to the organization and maintaining effective protection and recovery capabilities.
- Reporting to top management on security and controls.

Clearly the CIO/CISO is responsible for a large portion of the organization's system of internal controls, and must provide assurance to the CEO and CFO to enable them to comply with regulatory requirements.

The Auditor's Role in PC Control Structures

Internal auditors should include a review of PC controls as part of every audit, and should ensure that PC control issues are communicated to end users and integrated into the overall control process. The framework for audit assurance is made up of a set of audit methodologies and activities that can be used to facilitate, influence, and assess an organization's security program.

In addition to core security audits, the internal audit group can engage in a variety of facilitation activities, such as control self-assessments and surveys that target the PC environment. Questions in these surveys can be designed to improve overall awareness of critical PC security issues for a variety of target groups. They also provide internal audit teams with useful information for understanding and shaping the security culture in their organization.

Many other types of reviews and approaches can be considered to encompass various components of the audit program. Some potential audit projects include:

- Enterprise PC Policy Assessment.
- Security Program Development Facilitation.
- Employee Security Policy and Data Protection Assessment.
- Enterprise and Network Security Capability Assessment.
- Network Risk, Security, and Architecture Assessment.
- Review of Enterprise Intrusion Monitoring Capabilities.
- Review of Enterprise Data Classification, Retention, Archiving, and Disposition Activities.

Levels of Assessment for PC Controls

A PC control assessment can be designed to focus on broad organizational concerns or narrow security issues pertaining to specific applications or business processes. In the first case it is called a breadth assessment, in the second a depth assessment. Both are necessary to develop a full understanding of an organization's internal controls. Both can also be broken down into smaller units so the auditor can provide assurance around a specific component.

Breadth Assessments

Breadth assessments provide an opportunity to develop a broad perspective and analysis across a number of related functions, processes, activities, and systems. This type of assessment typically identifies all the activities and PC control points related to a common set of management functions. An example would be an analysis of the control environment for gathering, consolidating, and leveraging customer data. Customer data is typically gathered from many sources and activities, and a wide variety of PCs and individuals are involved. Data may be accessed through different applications, both online and offline. It may also be stored in different places, and aggregated in one or more backend marketing databases. Information may be extracted from these databases into a master customer database that is maintained by an entirely different function.

In this example, there are numerous data risks and potential control points where the auditor might provide assessment and risk analysis. Areas such as policy, privacy statements, Web applications, telephone applications, backend databases, transfers of data, and uploads from remote locations should all be considered, along with any other factors pertinent to the particular environment. An assessment survey is often a good starting point, since it provides a relatively quick method for gathering information from the many parties involved.

Breadth assessments are appropriate to high-level risk assessment. The number of activities and systems that are included preclude detailed reviews of process, application, security, and information technology. However, they do provide a broad perspective on the types of risk the organization faces, along with useful information for constructing depth assessments that focus on key areas of concern.

Depth Assessments

A depth assessment is a vertical, detailed audit that focuses on a specific business function and related processes, activities, and systems. An approach is developed to evaluate the business control environment; security policies and practices; applications used to collect, process, or store data; infrastructure components; network and operating system configuration controls; and IT processes for managing systems and software. This level of detail can help to provide a complete assessment of risks and controls to understand the integrity of PC management within a given business unit or function.

Leveraging Limited Audit Resources

In some ways, PC management is like the Year 2000 issue. For most organizations, it spans a large number of businesses, processes, activities, and systems. Dedicated resources for addressing PC management issues may be constrained, or even nonexistent, and the magnitude and complexity of the task can be intimidating.

Control self-assessment can provide an opportunity to leverage audit knowledge across a broad set of organizational areas. Self-assessments may be performed in support of a corporate security group or CSO, or as a business facilitation effort. One approach is to develop a PC audit program, and then leverage personnel in each business or department to execute the program with or without internal audit assistance. A Web-based system can be ideal for leveraging limited resources to address high-risk issues. This approach provides a central, easily accessible resource for deploying audit programs and evaluating and sharing results.

Annual Documentation and Substantiation

For the annual assessment, management must have procedures to demonstrate they have designed and maintained an effective system of controls. The solution is documentation, documentation, and more documentation. All processes, control objectives, and control activities should be documented, along with evidence that demonstrates their effectiveness.

Substantiating evidence, such as PC system logs, help desk logs, etc., should be retained and accessible to auditors for a length of time in keeping with documentation requirements. One solution is to store relevant data in easily accessible storage systems for a full year to meet this requirement, then preserve them on tape for longer periods as appropriate. Another is to extend the duration of the audit process across the full year, so controls can be documented without storing large amounts of data for extended periods.

In addressing compliance issues and documentation, it is important to understand the goals, motivations, and power of the governing authority. In some cases, a major violation might simply result in a warning letter that points out weaknesses and stipulates a time frame for improvement. In others, the potential may exist for your business to be fined or constrained from doing business as usual. The more you understand about the larger social and business context, the better you can focus your efforts on the desired outcome.

Enterprise Call to Action

It is important to monitor and understand regulatory requirements. However, leading organizations will not let this become the key driver for improving internal controls in their PC or other environments. Instead, management should focus on continuously improving the areas addressed throughout this report, such as: software currency (including patches), information security, virus updates, 24/7 operations, and continuous monitoring of the control environment. If these key issues are addressed and an adequate control environment is in place, regulatory compliance will also be satisfied. Of course, some specific industry regulations, such as HIPAA, GLB, FDICIA, or Federal Energy Regulatory Commission (FERC), may require additional measures. In most cases, however, a good internal control structure will make it much easier to address these additional needs.

A software security patch policy — and similar PC controls — should be based upon industry best practices to mitigate potential liability. The details of such a policy would of course depend upon the circumstances of the particular company or organization, including security commitments that are made explicitly by contract.

See Chapter 6 for more information and recommendations on software patching.

To ensure comprehensive controls, a framework such as COSO should be used in setting up structures and establishing documentation standards. A periodic (annual) breadth assessment should be conducted to evaluate and validate compliance with regulatory requirements. An automated, in-depth monitoring process that includes the reporting of exceptions should be in place as part of the overall model.

CHAPTER 4 INFORMATION SECURITY AND APPROPRIATE USE

Introduction

> *"People think this is a minor problem, all I need to do is hire someone to come in to put up a firewall, all I need is to have password access. Wrong! It is not a minor problem, and it is not easily fixed. It takes constant attention and there is no silver bullet."*
>
> — U.S. presidential advisor Richard A. Clarke, National Coordinator for Security, Infrastructure Protection, and Counter-Terrorism, 2001

Information security is the number one issue for the American technology community, according to the results of the 2003 Top Technologies survey by the American Institute of Certified Public Accountants (AICPA). It took the lead spot in the same survey in 2001, and came in third in 2002. This is not a trend that is likely to change in the near future. IT security is a core business concern for many organizations. Security is mandated for certain regulated industries and closely watched for others that make up a nation's critical infrastructures. Security failures in critical infrastructures impact not only the organization but also other industries depending on such organizations — and potentially the national defense and economy. Moreover, security risks continue to increase in volume and complexity. In the annual survey of U.S. corporations and government agencies conducted by the FBI and Computer Security Institute, 90 percent of respondents detected computer security breaches in the past year.

Yet quantifying security risk is difficult and solutions are complex. Many businesses continue to rely on centralized network security solutions, such as corporate firewalls and intrusion detection systems. These are important components of an enterprise security framework. However, the proliferation of mobile PCs, wireless networking, and connected computing solutions continues to blur the boundaries of the enterprise network. With these advances, the concept of a security-hardened perimeter for the protection of systems and information within the organization has expanded. Network safeguards must operate in concert with trusted computing environments based on the security of platforms, systems software, and operating systems. Given the volume and diversity of PCs, notebooks, and handheld devices in the average organization, an effective risk mitigation program must pay close attention to the client infrastructure.

Virtually every aspect of PC fleet management has an impact on information security — from platform choices and software management to upgrade cycles and end-user education. Security also depends on the implementation and management of key security-focused technologies and processes, such as PC vulnerability scanning, software patching, virus protection, personal firewalls, user authentication, and the administration of access privileges. Perhaps the greatest challenge is that security must be maintained individually on every PC because a single weak link can put the whole infrastructure at risk, threaten core business assets, and entail hundreds of thousands of dollars in IT cleanup costs.

Even with the extensive media coverage of hacking, worms, and viruses in recent years, there is a general lack of understanding of the basic elements of information security and of the return on security investments. This chapter focuses on providing a framework for addressing information security and outlines some of the key issues related to the PC infrastructure. It builds on the widely accepted understanding that information security depends on the integrity, confidentiality, and availability of information, and is considered a subset of overall enterprise security, which includes the physical security of systems and facilities.

Additional Security Guidance from The IIA

Security solutions are complex. They involve interactions across the entire organization, up and down the management structure, and across organizational boundaries to key players outside the organization. The IIA's February 2001 report, *Information Security Governance: What Directors Need to Know*[1], addresses the governance and management perspectives on information security starting with the audit committee of the board of directors. It poses 10 questions directors should ask about security management, and provides guidance on ensuring the answers are appropriate for the organization.

Oversight

The board of directors should exercise rigorous oversight of information technology. Authoritative guidance is available in a publication titled *Information Security Oversight: Essential Board Practices,* a publication of the National Association of Corporate Directors, which was sponsored

[1]The Information Security Management and Assurance series, jointly produced by The IIA, the National Association of Corporate Directors, the U.S. Critical Infrastructure Assurance Office, and other supporting organizations consists of three reports. The first two are written for board members, and the third is for management below the board level. They are: *Information Security Management and Assurance: A Call to Action for Corporate Governance; Information Security Governance: What Directors Need to Know;* and *Building, Managing, and Auditing Information Security.*

by KPMG's Audit Committee Institute in collaboration with The IIA, The Critical Infrastructure Assurance Office, and the U.S. Department of Commerce (December 2001). The project was co-chaired by Thomas Horton and Charles Elson.

The executive summary of this report features the following recommendations:

Essential Practice 1: Place Information Security on the Board's Agenda

- Make information security a regular agenda item (annual at a minimum) at board meetings.
- Ask management to report regularly on the state of information security.
- Include information security in the board's risk management discussions.
- Learn about the company's information security risk management policy and procedures.

Essential Practice 2: Identify Information Security Leaders, Hold Them Accountable, and Ensure Support for Them

- Find out who is in charge of information security, and to whom the person reports.
- Identify the role and resources of the internal auditor with respect to information security.
- Ensure education for the individuals involved and for all employees.
- Consider asking management to review and test policies and procedures using the internal audit function, the external audit firm, and/or another qualified third party.

Essential Practice 3: Ensure the Effectiveness of the Corporation's Information Security Policy through Review, Approval, and, if Necessary, Initial Development with Management

- Review the corporation's existing information security policy, or, if there is no policy, help management to develop one.
- Review the company's internal controls with regard to information security.
- Working with management, identify the greatest risks to the company's information security resources.
- Ensure that the appropriate screens are in place for company contractors.

Essential Practice 4: Assign Information Security to a Key Committee and Ensure Adequate Support for that Committee

- Consider delegating information security to a qualified board-level committee that can devote the time to this task, and write information security oversight into the committee's charter.
- Consider information security a potential area for audit coverage.
- Involve the audit committee (with the help of the internal and/or external auditor) in reviewing policies and procedures.
- Make full use of the internal audit function in creating and following information security oversight policies.

Enterprise Risk and the PC Infrastructure

The PC infrastructure continues to increase in importance to information security. One reason is the high volume of business and personal information that resides on PCs, notebooks, PDAs, and even phones. Engineers, accountants, executives, and many other employee classes often store sensitive information on their systems. In today's connected environment, any device may be the target of a digital attack that results in the theft or corruption of that information. Mobile devices pose somewhat greater risks, since they are often connected to the Internet from locations outside the corporate firewall. They are also more vulnerable to theft, especially if left unattended in an airport or other public location.

What makes client devices even more critical to information security is that a compromised system can provide a gateway into the network, which can put core business assets at risk. A digital threat, such as a virus or worm, can spread through the network from a single infected e-mail. There is also the danger of hacker infiltration. A common ploy is to take advantage of known vulnerabilities in popular Web browsers to install a backdoor application into a user's PC. The back door then automatically initiates a connection to the hacker's system and the hacker is notified of his success. He can then capture the user's keystrokes, including their user name and passwords. With this strategy, a hacker can literally take over a user's system, gaining access to everything available to the victim.

Viruses, Worms, and Other Threats

> **Note:** Viruses, worms, and similar threats are well covered in available publications and are not given in-depth treatment in this report. Rather, the impacts of these threats are addressed in the context of PC security management.

Anyone who even occasionally reads or listens to the news knows the incidence of cyber attacks has been increasing steadily over the last several years. The Computer Emergency Response Team Coordination Center (CERT CC) indicates the number of security incidents reported in the first half of 2003 (76,404) is very close to the total incidents reported for all of 2002 (82,094); and the number reported in 2002 was 56 percent greater than in 2001. If incidents continue at the current rate, the 2003 total will increase 86 percent over 2002.

The impact of a single attack can be substantial. In August 2003, the Welchi, or Nachi, worm infected 72,000 computers used by the U.S. Navy and Marine Corps and crippled Air Canada's reservation counters and call centers. CSX Transportation said a virus infection had slowed its dispatching and signal systems, forcing it to halt passenger and freight train traffic, including the morning commuter train service in Washington, D.C. A denial of service attack can target specific Web sites or systems with an army of "zombie" machines that can overpower system and network capacity, disrupt network services, and crash individual systems.

A worm such as SoBig can turn thousands of PCs around the world into spam machines. When a newly discovered vulnerability is exploited by such a worm, actions are required across a broad spectrum and may include such steps as those taken by America Online Inc., which blocked about 11.5 million message copies in the first day. SoBig.F hit the computing world as corporations were still recovering from several other worms, including the Blaster worm that spread through holes in Microsoft Corporation's Windows operating systems. It infected and crashed hundreds of thousands of computers in less than a week. Most of these attacks are difficult to trace to their origin. They are also becoming significantly more sophisticated as blended worms, spam, and other techniques are combined to increase the speed of propagation and the virulence of the attack.

The time frame between the announcement of a vulnerability from Microsoft and the release of a worm or virus exploiting that vulnerability continues to decrease. Even more problematic is the large volume of vulnerable systems that remain attached to the Internet long after corrective software patches have been made available.

Considerations for PC Security

Fundamental advances in PC platform security have been underway for several years, and the recent generation of platforms, operating systems, applications, and management tools enable better security at lower costs than was possible with older systems. They also interoperate more effectively with standards-based solutions for network security, which helps to simplify implementation and improve overall security. The key is to combine existing technologies effectively to establish a comprehensive, standards-based security solution that is both efficient and extensible.

The following are key factors in establishing information security for individual PCs. However, PC security also depends on the overall health and agility of the entire client infrastructure. The implementation of comprehensive best practices for PC management is therefore as important to security as it is to cost reduction. For that reason, many of the issues related below are discussed in more detail in other chapters of this report.

- **Software Currency and Patch Management:** Security analysts estimate approximately 90 percent of digital attacks target known vulnerabilities in popular applications and operating systems. It is therefore essential to actively monitor published vulnerabilities and distribute appropriate patches made available by software vendors. Standard hardware and software configurations and automated software distribution tools are important components of this process.

See Chapter 6 for more information.

- **Anti-virus and Personal Firewalls:** These applications are essential for mobile systems that operate outside the protected network, and they add a useful layer of additional protection for systems within the network. New threats emerge constantly, so these applications must be closely managed to ensure up-to-date virus signatures and firewall profiles are in place.

- **Configuration Monitoring:** Patches and updates can be sent out over the network, but may not be properly installed in each PC. Moreover, end users may download vulnerable software or turn off key security functions to improve performance. Because of these issues, hardware and software configurations should be actively monitored over the network. It is generally recommended that vulnerability scans be performed at least weekly (daily is better) and a routine process be established for rapidly assessing published vulnerabilities. Assessments can include standard rating levels (crisis, high, moderate, low) with predetermined time lines for remediation (1 week, 1 month, 2 months, a quarter). It is also important to assign accountable organizations to implement the stipulated controls.

- **Encryption:** File encryption is becoming a best practice for mobile systems, so stored data is not accessible on a stolen notebook. Network encryption via virtual private networking (VPN) is also recommended for wireless systems. This is especially important if the systems are used to access the network from remote locations. However, wireless communications can typically be monitored from up to a half mile away using relatively inexpensive and inconspicuous equipment. For this reason, encryption is also recommended for sensitive wireless transmissions within the enterprise.

- **Performance:** Older PCs may not provide adequate performance when running security software in tandem with production applications. This can lead to users turning off security applications and putting the network at risk. In general, such systems should be retired.

- **Logging:** Newer operating systems, such as Windows 2000 or Windows XP, provide logging capabilities for auditing security events. This is important for compliance and forensic investigation, and for understanding attacks to resolve vulnerabilities and limit damage. Without logging capabilities, a hacker intrusion could go completely undetected. Even worse, the malicious actions performed by the attacker could be attributed to the authorized user, and there would be no audit trail for proving otherwise.

- **Security Policies and User Awareness:** An uninformed user can compromise network security in many ways, including faulty password management, opening a questionable e-mail, downloading vulnerable software, or leaving an unguarded system logged onto the network or a business application. Policies should be regularly reviewed and should cover current issues, such as software piracy, shareware, open source systems, unauthorized software, inappropriate content, remote PC connectivity, removal of company information, and the use of home computers for work purposes. Training should take place on a regular basis and include a signoff to validate awareness and due diligence.

  A balanced approach is recommended in constructing and enforcing policies, since the results can significantly impact employee satisfaction, information security, and potential liability. Policies and processes should also address the risk of malicious insiders accessing authorized information. Internal checks and balances are important and should be proportional to the value of the information and the associated risk of exposure or corruption.

- **Smart Card or Biometric User Authentication:** Network IDs and passwords are important security tools, but they can be stolen or spoofed. Depending on your organization's risk profile, stronger authentication methods may be appropriate. This is especially true for businesses seeking to simplify user access and reduce support costs by deploying authentication middleware, such as password management, single sign-on, or authentication management infrastructure (AMI) products. These tools can be valuable and cost-effective. However, they also enable access to more information with fewer security checks. Stronger authentication can mitigate this increased risk.

The Importance of an Integrated Security Framework

In today's connected environment, the majority of systems and business processes are dependent in some way on the PC infrastructure. Because of this, PC security is meaningless as an isolated reality. Network, server, physical, and operational security are also essential elements of overall enterprise security. PC security policies must be carefully integrated with these other elements, and enterprise security strategy must be driven from the highest levels of the organization. Key business decision makers should be involved in establishing and implementing security policy. Those who set the agenda for enterprise security should be the same individuals who control the investment and take responsibility for success.

Solid security solutions are possible today, as is demonstrated by the wide support for Internet-based transactions in sensitive financial markets. In general, businesses should take advantage of proven technologies and methods. Innovation should not be the goal of security programs, but rather careful implementation and integration of proven technologies backed by appropriate processes.

When evaluating your PC security environment, consider the following actions and practices in the context of your own industry, organization, and culture. There is no one-size-fits-all solution, but these recognized practices should help.

- **Risk Management:** Reducing enterprise risk can improve bottom-line performance by reducing material impacts resulting from exploited vulnerabilities. Benefits may also be reflected in reduced insurance premiums. To align security investments with business needs, a formal approach to risk management is recommended (see *Return on Investment for Security Spending* below). Security is not an all-or-nothing proposition, but a series of trade-offs, preferably based on quantitative analysis. Each organization must establish appropriate levels of security based on their unique environment and provide customers and/or associates with sufficient confidence that digital transactions are accurate, private, and performed only with trusted parties.

- **Security Assessments and Audits:** It is important to understand where and how you are vulnerable to potential threats, including both internal and external attacks. It can be useful to enlist an outside security consultant to provide expertise. You can also take advantage of freely available resources, such as the Center for Internet Security. CIS (www.CISecurity.org) provides methods and tools to improve, measure, monitor, and benchmark the security status of your Internet-connected systems and appliances, plus those of your business partners. CIS members identify security threats of greatest concern, then participate in the development of practical methods to reduce vulnerability. There is no substitute for periodic independent and objective audits.[2] Make sure internal audit stays in touch with the information security organization, and follow up on audit recommendations.

- **A Security Road Map:** A well-constructed plan can allow you to continuously reduce your vulnerability and increase the total value of your computing environment.

- **A Comprehensive Approach:** Strong security requires thoughtful implementation and ongoing management. An effective solution must address not only technology issues, but also people, processes, and policies. It should also be designed to support continuous improvement. This typically requires:

[2]A valuable resource is the AICPA/CICA Trust Services Principles and Criteria, including criteria relating to Security, Privacy, Availability, Confidentiality, and Processing Integrity. For further details see www.aicpa.org/trustservices.

- An accountable corporate security executive who can enlist active support from key business decision makers.
- Formal processes for managing, assessing, auditing, and upgrading security solutions and policies. Technology alone is not an answer.
- A dedicated response team with formal disaster recovery and business continuity plans that are regularly reviewed and tested. Ideally, they would be used to respond to daily events. Formal plans are useless unless the organization knows how to implement them when a real crisis hits.
- A dedicated team for tracking security issues on a daily basis, and for keeping tabs on new regulations and technology advances.
- Sensitivity to internal politics and external trends and developments. For example, new regulations or a particularly successful attack can open doors that might normally be closed, enabling substantial progress in a shorter time frame.

Quantifying Risk and Value

There are many reasons for implementing a strong security program, including the auditing of risk management and compliance and the protection of intellectual property and proprietary information. These issues are important and should be key to justifying the value of security investments. However, they must ultimately be linked to bottom-line value through return on investment analysis if security is to receive funding in relationship to its value. IT security investments are increasingly being held to the same standard as other investments, and it is incumbent upon IT management to introduce analytical rigor into their decision-making process. To justify initial efforts, it can be instructive to look at industry norms for the cost of security breaches. However, an effective long-term strategy will require a more customized analysis of the return on investment for security spending in your particular organization.

The Cost of Security Breaches

Most organizations are understandably reluctant to share information about serious security events, since a publicized breach can impair their reputation and may raise serious trust issues with customers and business collaborators. It can therefore be difficult to obtain reliable financial information regarding the impact of security breaches, and estimates have varied considerably.

A recent research study by Ashish Garg, Ph.D., Jeffrey Curtis, and Hilary Halper of Ernst & Young LLP's Business Analytics Practice sheds light on this important issue by quantifying the impact of security incidents on stock price. It also explores the impact on stock price of information security spending. The results were published in "The Financial Impact of IT Security Breaches: What Do Investors Think," *Information Systems Security*, March/April 2003. A series of articles in the ITAudit.org Forum also addresses the financial implications of security breaches and the return on security investments. See Information Security Governance, ITAudit Forum, February 15, 2001, at www.ITAudit.org.

These sources indicate the actual costs of security events are actually greater than previously estimated, and a single event can cost millions of dollars. Any meaningful reduction in risk or damage can therefore readily justify the cost of a sizable security program. Of course, such studies provide only general metrics that may not apply to specific businesses. However, they do provide a useful starting point, and can provide business justification for establishing a security program that can address the fundamental technical and financial issues that are unique to each organization.

Evaluating Return on Investment for Security Spending

Assessing the value of specific security investments begins by quantifying the value and vulnerability of key corporate assets — such as customer data, intellectual property, financial information, production systems, etc. — along with the potential loss that would be caused by damage or theft. The analysis must also take into account the threat matrix in today's connected environment, and the costs and risk mitigation potential of each investment.

Jeff Curtis, a senior consultant in Ernst & Young's Economics & Business Analytics practice, has outlined a Value of Risk Avoidance methodology (VoRA) to assess the Return on Security Investments (ROSI). VoRA provides a practical approach to assessing the types of threats and their expected frequency and impacts on employees and business assets. It uses this information to quantify the value of risk avoidance in comparison with specific security program costs. As noted in the previous section, security breeches will ultimately affect the stock price. VoRA complements stock-focused analysis by identifying and quantifying both tangible and intangible precursors to reduced market valuation, including:

- Loss of productivity.
- Loss of revenue.
- IT support costs.
- Cost of system repair/replacement.
- Cost of insurance.
- Impact on brand and reputation.
- Loss of trading partner confidence.
- Increased regulatory risk.
- Legal implications.

Curtis also addresses some key factors that impact an organization's risk profile, such as the:

- Structure of the organization.
- Number and types of employees likely to be impacted.
- Distribution of employees and company information.
- Industry regulatory environment.

A detailed evaluation of these factors can help security administrators understand and quantify the value of specific security enhancements. By comparing the costs of proposed projects and establishing criteria for prioritization of security projects, they can build a credible and defensible business case for the new security initiatives.

When performing this evaluation, it is important to understand security variables and metrics in terms of the organization's larger goals and issues. Understanding the specific industry, including which tangible and intangible costs are most relevant, is important to build and maintain credibility with business and financial decision makers.

Of course, risk avoidance is not the only justification for security investments. New technologies and methods may also produce substantial efficiency gains. Security vendors are focused on the need for more integrated and manageable solutions. This is certainly true for PC-related security issues. Today's automated asset management, security scanning, and software distribution tools can greatly reduce the cost of monitoring, updating, and auditing the PC environment. In some cases, it may be cheaper and more effective to install new solutions than to manage current systems. These effects should be included in the financial assessment.

Though unavoidably complex during initial use, a formal approach to ROSI can be instrumental in justifying and implementing an appropriate security program, and in tying program development to business value. For most organizations, the benefits will increase substantially with time as analysts identify, track, and refine the key metrics in their particular environment.

For more information about ROSI, visit The IIA's Web site at: http://www.theiia.org/esac/index.cfm?fuseaction=or&page=rciap.

Technology Innovation and Appropriate Use

Connected computing, wireless mobility, and Internet-based commerce offer significant opportunity and competitive advantage for most organizations, yet each of these technologies has also introduced new security risks. In general, this trade-off exists for virtually any technology that simplifies and improves access to valuable information. PC security issues increased dramatically with the advent of networking and the Internet. Yet the decision of whether to take advantage of these capabilities is a non-issue for the majority of organizations. As with many new PC-related technologies today, the competitive value is simply too great to ignore.

The real challenge for business and IT leaders, therefore, is to deploy new technologies judiciously and to extend existing security solutions as needed based on careful analysis of risks and benefits. Important issues include the existence and reliability of industry standards for the new technology, and the effectiveness and cost-effectiveness of existing security solutions.

Wireless mobility offers an instructive example. The rapid growth of wireless attests to its productivity benefits, which analysts have estimated at up to 11 hours a week for a professional with a wireless notebook (as opposed to a non-wireless notebook). Early wireless security standards proved too weak for enterprise needs. However, existing technologies, such as virtual private networking (VPN), can be extended to wireless applications, providing time-tested methods for encryption and user authentication.

Such solutions must be carefully integrated with existing enterprise security frameworks. For example, best practices for wireless security typically include scanning for rogue systems and segmenting the wireless network from the trusted network so only authenticated users can access core business information. Of course, wireless security standards continue to improve. Businesses that wait will probably have more cost-effective security options available. However, they will lose the competitive advantages of early adoption, which may be substantial — and they will still have to invest in establishing a comprehensive and well-integrated security solution. Better security standards will undoubtedly deliver incremental value, but may not be worth the delay.

In general, businesses should monitor emerging technologies and carefully evaluate potential value, along with the cost and risk of implementation. There is an increasing convergence between computing and communication devices, which can increase flexibility, mobility, and ease of information access. Current examples include wireless PDAs and other wireless handheld devices, instant messaging, "ad hoc" networking, and voice-over IP (VOIP). Ad hoc networking enables the direct connection between two devices, with no server in between to monitor (and safeguard) communications. VOIP enables voice communications to be transmitted across standard data networks.

These and other emerging technologies offer new capabilities and solutions that may improve communication and productivity. Some are simple enough to be implemented by employees using free downloadable software or widely available consumer products. This is a relatively common scenario — and a good reason for business and security executives to carefully evaluate new technologies, establish policies, and control their deployment within the organization.

The COSO model provides a good framework for assessing the control environment, but must be adapted by each organization to fit the culture, risk appetite, and strategy for adopting new technology. Only those organizations that are unlikely to read a report such as this would even consider preventing the adoption and use of popular new technologies as a viable solution.

Evaluating Security for New Products and Technologies
As part of its increased focus on security, Microsoft Corporation introduced the following criteria for assessing product security. It can be a useful model for evaluating PC technology and product innovations, and provides important insights for security and IT decision makers. In general, all IT products should be:

- **Secure by Design:** Security should no longer be an afterthought in product design. Look for standards-based tools and services that specifically address security issues and can be integrated effectively into your own security framework. Products that are designed for security are likely to support better solutions at lower costs.

- **Secure by Default:** The industry has long focused on convenience and ease-of-use at the expense of security. One example was the enormous number of built-in services that were turned on by default in older operating systems, such as Windows NT 4.0 and Windows 98. Many of these services were unnecessary for most PC users, and some would only be needed in a server environment. Such activated but unused services add no value, but can substantially increase vulnerability. Today, services that may not be required should be turned off by default, and it should require active configuration by an informed user to turn them on.

- **Secure by Deployment:** This requires the deployment of comprehensive best practices as discussed in this chapter and throughout this report. Look for products and vendors that provide clear documentation of the security concerns and potential solutions that relate directly to their offerings.

Enterprise Call to Action

Security has been described as a race without a finish. It involves managing many diverse factors, such as perceptions and misconceptions, awareness and apathy, protection versus ease of use and access, compliance and effective practices, return on security investments, and enterprise risk management. It involves dealing with rapidly changing rules, threats, vulnerabilities, and strategies. Effective protection today may be negated by tomorrow's technology advances and/or the discovery of new vulnerabilities in software, systems, and networks.

In short, there is no simple way to protect your PC infrastructure — and your enterprise — from digital threats. However, strong and efficient security is possible today. For most organizations, an effective solution requires a comprehensive security policy and road map, a formal approach to risk management and ROI, continuous monitoring and assessment of threats and events, strong and immediate recovery capabilities, and regular security assessments.

In establishing and maintaining effective PC security, priority should be given to industry-standard security technologies that provide a flexible foundation for integration and growth. Improving the efficiency of patch management processes and keeping your PC and server infrastructure up-to-date are among the most cost-effective steps toward enhancing security. Regular PC refreshes and automated platform management tools help to ensure a consistent computing environment with the power and functionality to support increasing security and application requirements.

Organizations should also consider the automated management tools offered by leading PC manufacturers and software vendors. As discussed elsewhere in this report, advanced tools based on industry standards can deliver significant advantages in asset management, platform security management, standard configuration enforcement, software updates, and fault management. Though some of these factors are not directly related to security concerns, they increase your ability to respond quickly and effectively to remediate emerging threats.

As stated previously, the COSO framework is a widely accepted model for internal control, and is recommended for addressing controls at the PC level. Keep in mind that a single security breech can cost millions of dollars, which could cover the entire budget for a large security program. Audit committees should specifically address the adequacy of resources provided for security, and should seek confirmation from internal audit.

CHAPTER 5
BUSINESS CONTINUITY AND THE PC

Introduction

The PC has become thoroughly integrated into the majority of job functions in most large organizations. Word processing, spreadsheets, presentation software, communications, and other mainstream applications are now essential productivity tools. Many job functions also rely on task-specific applications that run on general-purpose PCs. In most cases the data accessed by the PC, whether stored on the PC or on backend systems, is just as important as the PC hardware and software. If PC tools and information are not available, an employee's function may be impossible to perform efficiently — or at all. It is therefore important that appropriate tools and processes be in place to quickly and efficiently restore data and functionality for failed PCs.

Traditional contingency planning covers many aspects of business continuity, including recovery teams, action plans, equipment inventory, network and data center operations, transportation, forms and supplies, plan maintenance, alternate facilities, and testing. This chapter addresses only those areas specifically related to PC management in a networked environment. (For more details on the overall contingency management process, see *Systems Auditability and Control (SAC) Module 10, Contingency Planning,* by The IIA Research Foundation. *SAC* documents a comprehensive framework for overall contingency planning.)

An effective strategy for the recovery of one or more failed PCs begins with a detailed understanding of business objectives, processes, and risks. In most cases, an individual PC is not critical to the entire enterprise. However, if that PC is the sole link to a business-critical database or is used to control a major assembly line, its importance may be extremely high. Moreover, any networked machine can be the entry point for a virus or worm that will impact all systems on the network, and possibly bring down the network itself.

Business continuity at the PC level depends on two primary issues. The first is the recovery of individual machines. With proper tools and planning, this can be a quick and relatively painless process. The second is the recovery of the network and all affected machines in the event of a virus infection or other large-scale security event. This may require substantial coordination across the enterprise to ensure key systems, network segments, and business processes are quickly restored and properly protected against further infection.

The Role of the PC Architecture

Architectural decisions can have a significant impact on PC operations and recoverability. Three primary PC architectures exist in information networks today. The most common is the traditional fat client architecture in which each PC has its own hard drive, is configured to host complete applications, and can store both software and data. The mobile client architecture is similar, but presents special issues for maintenance, support, and recovery. A third option is the thin client model. In this case, the end-user device is primarily a user interface that accesses processing power, applications, and data from networked servers that typically support multiple clients.

In terms of system management and recovery, the thin client is probably the most efficient, followed by the fat client, and then the mobile PC. Of course, productivity issues are critical in choosing the best architecture for a particular business and function, which accounts for the increasing popularity of mobile systems despite a somewhat higher total cost of ownership. The discussion below is applicable primarily to fat client architectures and mobile PCs — the most popular solutions at this time.

Restoring Individual PCs

Almost anyone who has worked with PCs over an extended period of time has experienced a system crash due to a hard drive failure or some other software or hardware related issue. At best, there are work delays as the problem is resolved. At worst, there can be lost data that represents hours, weeks, or even months of lost productivity.

In the survey conducted for this research project, a mere 40 percent of respondents reported their organizations backed up PC data in a central location. A larger percentage, 47 percent, reported having a full image backed up for PC recovery. (An image includes the operating system and all major applications and settings.) In general, a full image backup should be considered a best practice for PC management, especially for job functions that require recovery time frames of less than 24 hours. With today's best tools, a failed PC can be re-imaged and its data reloaded within a few hours, and this process can be performed over the network from a remote location. Of course, for hardware-related problems, additional measures may be required. New components may have to be installed or a replacement PC deployed.

Most organizations will differentiate recovery processes to some extent based on the importance of the individual PC. For example, on the trading floor of a financial institution, every individual may have two or three fully operable PCs due to the significant loss of revenue that could result from a trader being unable to perform. Individuals in less critical capacities may be expected to wait several hours for system restoration using the processes described above. Others could reasonably expect to wait a week or more for a new PC to be ordered, configured, and installed.

Risk versus TCO

In evaluating policies, tools, and processes, total cost of ownership should be a key consideration. If automated image and data restoration are implemented for some systems, it will be incrementally less costly to extend those capabilities to other systems. In addition, quick automated processes can greatly decrease the burden on help desk and support staff, and also reduce the level of expertise required to perform recovery operations.

For most organizations, it will not be cost-effective to have a fully configured backup PC for every individual in case of hardware failure. Yet a number of partially imaged PCs can be kept in reserve at key locations, ensuring quick replacement machines for a large number of users. In conjunction with the automated image and data recovery tools already mentioned, this can reduce recovery times significantly, even for hardware-damaged systems. An inventory of key components may also be advisable. This enables failed hardware to be replaced more quickly and returned to the user or to a central repository for redeployment.

Backup frequency is another important issue in centralized PC recovery solutions. For mobile PCs that only occasionally connect to the network, it may be appropriate to perform a backup each time a connection is made. For desktops and laptops that are frequently or always connected, timing is a function of policy. Frequent backups minimize potential data loss, but also create additional overhead and increase network bandwidth requirements. The decision to perform backups hourly, annually, or somewhere in between should be based on a quantitative analysis of value at risk and the total cost of the solution.

Notebook Challenges

Notebook (or laptop) PCs present additional challenges for rapid recovery when individuals are away from a central location. Automated data and image restoration is still possible, but bandwidth constraints will most likely slow the process significantly. Today's best tools are able to adjust to bandwidth limitations, and can smoothly continue restoration in the event a connection is lost and reestablished. Spare parts and replacement systems for travelers can be a more difficult challenge. Some organizations have established contracts with their suppliers to drop-ship a new system to any location within 24 hours in the event of PC failure.

24/7 PC Support

Most enterprises have a centralized help desk to support users with PC-related problems. These facilities often provide various levels of support and typically help to resolve software issues over the phone. Help desk personnel typically have detailed procedures for addressing various PC problems. The integration of help desk applications with network-based asset management and PC restoration tools can substantially accelerate average resolution times and improve the percentage of issues that can be handled remotely. Centrally administered PC support can also help provide a central nexus for tracking and analyzing PC problems and support efficiency.

Testing

The processes involved in recovering individual PCs are tested daily in a large enterprise. Data should be collected and reviewed regularly to identify common problems or recurring user issues, and metrics should be devised for tracking and understanding related costs and service levels. Problems should be summarized by category, and root cause analysis should be used to identify problematic vendors, models, components, applications, etc. If recovery of an individual's data is not possible, causes should be reviewed and action taken to avoid future occurrences, since even a single event can be costly, depending on the data and its value.

The Issue of Responsibility

A project manager worked for a large retailer, and over five years accumulated data for several critical projects on her hard drive. Company policy called for information services to back up the image and data for every PC on a regular basis. She depended on this policy and practice. However when her hard drive failed, it turned out that her system had not been properly backed up over the full five-year period.

Should the project manager have relied on the system of internal controls, or should she have taken responsibility for backing up her own data occasionally? Should she have at least periodically tested the backup and recovery process?

There are no easy answers. However, it is clear that the existence of a centralized backup solution may reduce the extent to which individuals take responsibility for their own backups. Internal controls are essential, and end-users and internal organizations should be given some indication of the rigor of those controls. They should also be informed that no backup system is infallible. In all cases, the value of systems and data should be carefully considered, and redundant backup solutions should be implemented as appropriate.

Specific and regular recovery testing should be implemented for PCs involved in all critical business functions. These tests should be integrated into corporate and departmental recovery tests to ensure procedures will work together under foreseeable scenarios. Root cause analysis should be performed to resolve any recovery issues that arise during these tests.

Recovering the Network and Connected Systems

As previously addressed in this report, a computer worm can impact traffic on the network and impair enterprise operations. It is generally more efficient to protect against infection than to recover from it, so appropriate safeguards are essential. *(See Chapters 4 and 6 for more information.)* However, when an infection occurs, quick and effective action can potentially save thousands or millions of dollars, minimizing operational downtime and reducing cleanup and recovery costs.

Network recovery can be a highly complex process, and is beyond the scope of this report. However, from a high-level perspective, processes should be in place for monitoring the network and individual systems for infection. Dedicated personnel should track key security sites for early warnings about vulnerabilities and real or possible attacks. For most vulnerabilities, software patches are available, or software and/or security vendors will quickly release appropriate updates and virus removal utilities. Depending on circumstances, it is highly advisable to test these updates and patches before deployment. However, in some cases, imminent risks may outweigh potential interoperability issues, and testing may not be appropriate.

Recovery teams should be ready to respond instantly. Roles and responsibilities should be understood. Action plans should take into account how the network is segmented as well as the business value associated with particular segments and connected systems. A well-designed recovery plan will efficiently recover the network and prioritize system restoration based on the value of supported business functions.

Disaster Recovery

A comprehensive plan should also be in place for recovering from large-scale disasters that incapacitate, damage, or destroy a substantial portion of the PC infrastructure. This plan should leverage the capabilities already discussed, such as online data and image backups, and agreements with vendors for delivering partially or fully imaged PCs on short notice. For this requirement, data and image backups should be stored off-site to ensure recoverability. Existing systems and processes should be assessed to understand how they will respond to the high-volume demands of large-scale recovery operations. This should include not only internal systems and controls, but also external resources, such as PC vendor capabilities and network bandwidth for image and data restoration.

Recovery staff should have a clear understanding of the number of PCs at all major locations, as well as their specific configurations and their relative priority in terms of the business processes they support. Plans for each location should also include communication procedures and recovery time frames. Disaster recovery plans, systems, and procedures should be tested regularly to ensure they are functioning properly and can handle projected workloads, which may change substantially over time for various locations.

The PC as a Contingency Solution

The PC can also serve as part of the solution in contingency planning. Notebooks in the field, in particular, can serve as offline storage devices, especially if they have data that is regularly synchronized with network servers or databases. In a number of cases, notebooks have proven valuable for businesses recovering from power outages and server crashes. Of course, these capabilities depend on synchronization with other data sources in the enterprise. Careful planning can provide the enterprise with off-site data backup and relatively easy recovery for critical information.

PCs should also be considered as a valuable processing resource, especially during a disaster in which other systems may not be available. These capabilities can be especially important with respect to departmental disaster scenarios, and contingency planners and internal auditors should be aware of the possibilities. Management should also consider working with vendors to provide the ability to provide pre-configured standard machines to any location within the enterprise within a predefined time (i.e., 24 or 48 hours). These types of contracts can be extremely useful in disaster scenarios and are provided for at a reasonable cost.

Enterprise Call to Action

Contingency planning is essential for both individual PC restoration and network restoration. The following is a summary of key actions that help ensure a rapid response and quick recovery.

- Establish standard recovery times for various functions based on specific problem categories and criticality.
- Monitor performance for PC support and recovery processes, and document processes for network recovery.
- Have each PC user and business function perform a risk assessment and establish recovery time objectives for their machine(s).
- Determine if any major changes should be made to the enterprise PC architecture (fat client, mobile client, thin client, or combination).

- Establish clear policies and methods for PC backup and recovery.
- Provide thorough testing of PC backup and recovery processes.
- Determine the optimal number and locations of spare machines based on user numbers and the criticality of business functions.

CHAPTER 6
SOFTWARE MANAGEMENT AND CURRENCY

Introduction

Effective software management is one of the most crucial aspects of a good PC fleet management strategy. A well-managed software environment is more stable, with fewer compatibility issues, better security, fewer help desk calls, and faster problem resolution.

The importance of software management was underlined by Aberdeen Group in their 2003 list of best practices for PC management. In prioritizing best practices by return on investment, two out of the top three recommendations — deploying standard software images and software distribution — focused on effective software management. Both of these processes can be substantially improved using automated, network-based tools. Both processes also rely on establishing a consistent PC environment based on well-defined organizational standards.

The Benefits of Standardization

In general, the more diverse the software environment, the more difficult and costly it is to manage and maintain. Most organizations will benefit from simplifying their environment by establishing a handful of PC configurations targeting specific user groups. Giga Information Group reports "the benefit of standardizing on four to six application configurations represents a 15 percent to 25 percent reduction in IT costs during the system life cycle (an average of $1,600 per system)."[1]

Standardization lays the foundation for efficient fleet management. With a consistent environment, many manual processes can be replaced or augmented with automated tools that enable fewer people to manage a large number of PCs. When deploying new PCs, systems can be powered up over the network. The operating system and applications can then be uploaded automatically — with minimal human intervention. Software updates and security patches can also be distributed over the network. Standardization also improves help desk support. Since the PC support staff encounters fewer variations, common problems can be identified and resolved more quickly.

---

[1]Kriebel Norbert, and William Sheehan, *The Economics of Client-Systems Standardization* (Giga Information Group, March 26, 2001).

Of course, efforts at standardization must be carefully balanced against end-user productivity needs. An engineer, an accountant, and a manufacturing supervisor may have very different application requirements. Moreover, some organizations — universities are one example — are simply not in a position to standardize all the PCs that access their network. Every organization must seek the appropriate balance between uncontrolled diversity and a single, locked-down PC configuration. The ability to accurately find this balance is crucial to implementing an effective PC management strategy.

A standardized environment can present a different type of risk. In our research we noted a number of large enterprises that were negatively impacted by a major vulnerability or error in a distributed software change. These companies were impacted across the entire enterprise due to the "ripple effect" of a single change in a homogeneous environment. Other PC computing environments did not experience the same level of impact, because they did not have a standard PC environment. Although the total cost ownership (TCO) model for these highly diverse environments is much higher — including the cost of distributing software changes — the impact of a single event on the overall environment could be less. Of course, there are many ways to mitigate risk in a standardized environment, including comprehensive testing, segmentation of the enterprise network, piloting changes prior to applying them to the enterprise, and well-thought-out contingency plans.

Reducing Software Configuration Changes with Stable Platforms

Since many components of a PC's operating software interact directly with the hardware components, different hardware configurations will often be unable to run the same software image. Standardizing the software environment therefore requires standardizing the hardware environment.

Large organizations typically standardize on a small number of desktop and mobile hardware configurations, then develop and qualify a standard software image for each configuration. Once an image is qualified, any change to the standard hardware configuration can "break" the image, creating serious interoperability issues. Since a typical PC includes dozens of components from many different vendors, component upgrades are common. This has been a major problem for large organizations with thousands of PCs; forcing them to reengineer and re-qualify images any time their PC vendor issues a component change in one of their standard configurations.

To address this issue, leading PC vendors now offer "stable platforms" that specifically target the needs of large businesses to minimize changes to qualified configurations. Large organizations are encouraged to work closely with their PC vendor to understand the advantages and limitations of stable platforms. With close cooperation, they can time their platform and image qualifications to coincide with the release of new stable platforms by their vendor(s). This will enable them to take advantage of a given configuration for a longer period, and reduce the number of qualifications they have to perform.

The Volatility of PC Operating Software

Today's PC operating systems are highly complex, with millions of lines of code and an extensive assortment of services and capabilities. The PC operating system (OS) acts as the intermediary between the PC hardware and software. It is a critical component — and it is constantly changing. Change comes from two key sources: major version upgrades, and ongoing patches and service packs, which are made available by vendors to address security and interoperability issues that arise in the interval between version releases. A key question for IT organizations is how often they should upgrade their PC operating systems, and how thorough they should be in deploying patches and updates.

Keeping Operating Systems Current

Compatibility with evolving applications and hardware components is one reason to deploy current operating system versions. Businesses relying on out-of-date OS versions may run into complications when they try to upgrade other applications or services in their infrastructure. OS upgrades may also introduce useful features that can help to solve certain challenges. For example, Microsoft Windows 2000/XP includes enhanced support for several security functions, such as file encryption, virtual private networks (VPN), and smart card authentication. Using these features can be cost-effective, since they are included at no extra charge and automatically available in all systems running that particular OS. Of course, businesses may have existing solutions, or they may find that third-party applications offer essential features that are not included in the OS implementation. Or they may simply not be interested in the enhanced feature set of a new OS version.

In general, every IT organization must evaluate OS version upgrades based on expected benefits versus the cost of migrating to the new version — including planning, hardware upgrades or replacements, software migration, and follow-on support costs. However, the importance of upgrading becomes critical when operating systems reach an age when they are no longer supported by the vendor. Out-of-date operating systems are particularly vulnerable to digital attack, since the vendor no longer provides patches for newly discovered security vulnerabilities. As noted by META Group, *"...the complexity and breadth of an OS makes running without vendor support a high risk."*[2]

---

[2]Kleynhans, Steve, "The Final Push to Windows 2000," Meta Group, February 14, 2003.

Organizations running Microsoft Windows operating systems should be aware that Microsoft no longer supports Windows NT 4.0* and support for Windows 98* is scheduled to end on January 16, 2004.[3] In response to this, META Group recommends *"...organizations plan to finalize the migration [to Windows 2000/XP] by YE2003 or face significant operational issues in 2004."*[4] According to analysts at Giga Information, IT functions should also look closely at the support available for other applications in their PC environment. They caution that any unsupported software increases risk and delivers less value to the enterprise.[5]

The Value of Effective Controls

Independent (unpublished) research by Gene Kim, CTO of Tripwire, Inc., and Kevin Behr, CTO and chief operational strategist of IP Services, Inc., indicates best-in-class organizations realize significant financial and efficiency benefits from effective control practices. For example, organizations with large server farms have been able to improve their server to system administrator ratio to as much as 250/1 by employing techniques such as repeatable builds for their servers (a standard configuration that is deployed across a large number of systems). By contrast, organizations with weak control structures may have a server/sysadmin ratio of only 10/1. In addition to the improved efficiency of personnel, the reliability of servers and the time required for recovery from failures are also greatly improved. Similar benefits are gained by efficiently managing the configuration and deployment of PCs. With a homogeneous and well-controlled PC infrastructure, the frequency and complexity of help desk and other support functions are decreased; software patching is greatly simplified; and the time required for recovery from system failures and other disruptions is substantially decreased.

The Challenge of Software Security Patching

Security analysts estimate over 90 percent of digital threats attack known software vulnerabilities in PC or server platforms. In most cases, vendors are aware of these vulnerabilities and have already developed software patches to address them. Yet IT functions can be overwhelmed with the pure volume of updates, along with the complexity of resolving dependencies and ensuring application and platform readiness as they engineer, qualify, test, and distribute these patches. Nevertheless, as stated in the Steptoe & Johnson, LLP paper "A Patch in Time Saves Nine:

---

[3]For more information, visit the Microsoft Web site at: http://www.microsoft.com/windows/lifecycle/desktop/business/default.mspx
[4]Kleynhans, Steve, "The Final Push to Windows 2000," Meta Group, February 14, 2003.
[5]Miller, Byron, "Don't Use Unsupported Software," Giga Information Group, Inc., February 20 2003.

Liability Risks for Unpatched Software:" "It is largely undisputed that the effort and expense of installing security patches is generally less than the effort and expense of recovering from attacks that exploit unpatched vulnerabilities."

Software Patching in Protected Networks

A key objective of software patching is to correct software vulnerabilities. But patching is only one element of a secure environment, and a software patch may not be needed if other controls prevent access to vulnerable software.

Firewalls, virus protection, change management, monitoring, and user authentication are examples of controls that work together to provide security. Secure environments include preventive, detective, and corrective controls. Because controls are not infallible, secure environments also have redundant controls so a failure of one control will be detected by another.

Software security patches are most critical in Internet-facing systems that perform sensitive business functions and/or provide access to sensitive information. PCs with e-mail capability as well as access to other business systems and information represent a potential vulnerability and should have a high priority for security patching. They may also serve as a gateway for introducing harm to other network components.

A Growing Concern

Microsoft and other software vendors have significantly increased their focus on security issues. Yet the combination of software complexity, multiple deployed versions, and a very active hacker community ensures that new security issues will continue to emerge. The increased industry focus on security also has a downside. Increased scrutiny leads to the discovery of more flaws, which are published by the security community. Hackers also have access to these published lists. As a result, vulnerabilities are being exploited with increasing speed, forcing software vendors and businesses to react faster. For example, the SQL Slammer worm took eight months to appear after the vulnerability was announced. Blaster appeared after only one month.

Digital threats are also becoming more sophisticated. Today's blended worms, for example, are designed to attack and propagate in multiple ways. Some can spread globally in a matter of minutes, rather than days. They also do more damage and are more difficult to clean up.

The Patch Process

> The CERT Coordination Center at Carnegie Mellon University is the respected source of information on security vulnerabilities. Similar information is also available from other sources, including the U.S. Department of Homeland Security ("DHS"), which maintains information on security vulnerabilities through its Information Analysis and Infrastructure Protection Directorate[6] and has recently announced a collaboration with CERT to create the U.S. Computer Emergency Response Team ("US-CERT").[7]

As the Steptoe & Johnson paper indicates, patch management "is not necessarily a straightforward process. Even for large companies and organizations that have personnel tasked with implementing patches, problems include ensuring that patches (1) are deployed to every affected computer and (2) are compatible with the organization's existing computing environment. The first issue is a difficult one in organizations with many thousands of computers, and is particularly serious given that a single unpatched computer can threaten the security of a network. On the second issue, most network administrators have tales to tell about patches that fixed a hole but broke the network, or at least certain applications. Even Microsoft recognizes that there is some risk of disruption when a user installs one of its patches:

Rollback considerations. Can a release be uninstalled? Are necessary provisions in place in the event a computer stops responding after a patch is deployed? Are the proper data backup and restore procedures taking place? Understanding the requirements for returning computers to their original state in the unlikely event that a deployment adversely affects your environment is an important aspect of release management.[8]"

There is no simple solution to this challenge. Among both analysts and users, there are those who advocate the extremes of not patching at all, and those who advocate comprehensive patching to stay current at all times. Neither of these strategies will work for most businesses. Failing to deploy critical patches can have serious consequences. Yet the cost of testing and deploying every patch for every application is generally prohibitive.

---

[6]*See* http://www.dhs.gov/dhspublic/interapp/editorial/editorial_0335.xml.

[7]*See* "Secretary Ridge Announces the Creation of New Computer Emergency Response Center for Cyber Security," DHS press release (Sept. 15, 2003).

[8]*The Microsoft Guide to Security Patch Management*, p. 113, available at http://www.microsoft.com/technet/treeview/default.asp?url=/technet/security/topics/patch/secpatch/Default.asp (2003).

The recommended solution lies in establishing effective risk management procedures for analyzing vulnerabilities and determining the best course of action. It is important to have a formal system in place, with standard processes and authorizations. Each business must understand the value of their IT assets and the vulnerability of their network and systems to digital attacks, including viruses, worms, Trojans, hackers, denial of service, and internal misuse or abuse of resources. With this information, they can monitor new threats and more quickly evaluate their risk exposure based on their unique technical and business considerations. With a formal system in place, the risk of not deploying a patch can quickly be weighed against the costs and risk of deploying it. Some patches should be distributed as soon as possible, others can be grouped for later distribution, and others may be installed only as part of a service pack or software version upgrade.

In general, a patch management policy should involve at least the following elements:

- Implementation of available patches to address vulnerabilities that are (1) publicly identified by CERT (and/or other sources, such as DHS) and/or (2) noted by the relevant software manufacturer;
- Policies and processes to ensure that such implementation takes place on a timely basis, subject to deployment concerns — e.g., ensuring compatibility of patches with the existing computing environment and pursuing alternatives if compatibility issues are identified;
- Rapid replacement of software, particularly software that has significant known security vulnerabilities (identified by CERT, the manufacturer, or other sources) for which patches are not available; and
- Specific implementation of statutory and/or regulatory requirements applicable in a given sector (especially health care or financial services).

Several additional steps are also generally advisable:

1. **Implement regular security scanning** to identify vulnerable systems and audit the security environment. Analysts at Gartner recommend IT functions scan all systems at least weekly, and move toward daily scans.[9] Scanning is important to make sure patches are not only distributed, but successfully installed. Frequent scanning can also help ensure end users have not compromised network security by downloading vulnerable software from the Internet, or turning off security applications, such as virus scanning or personal firewalls. Ideally, this scanning function should be independent of patch distribution processes to provide an effective audit of the PC security environment. (One method is to use an off-the-shelf, agent-based management system for patch distribution, and use OS-based tools and services for independent configuration scanning.)

[9]Pescatore, J., *Update Your Internet Server Security,* Gartner Research Note, 2003.

2. **Standardize on a handful of client configurations.** This is one of the most effective ways to limit patching complexity and enable adequate testing in a reasonable time frame. However, it should be mentioned that some analysts and users recommend the opposite. They prefer a diverse base of PCs that make it hard for a worm or virus to find a consistent flaw across the infrastructure, and may therefore impede propagation. However, such an environment may be prohibitively costly to manage, and may foster a diverse range of potential vulnerabilities that ultimately will make it more likely for one or more PCs to be compromised, thus putting the network at risk.

3. **Create an isolated test environment** for quickly testing new patches. This should include a set of systems that mirror your deployed PC configurations. You should also have a standard set of tests to ensure testing consistency. When appropriate, the scope of the tests can be varied based on the severity and urgency of the security threat.

4. **Deploy automated tools for network-based software distribution,** and explore the advantages of automated patch management applications. Effective tools can accelerate distribution, making it easier to stay current with the most critical patches.

Industry Shift Ahead?

Because of the wide deployment of its software, Microsoft Corporation is one of the main sources for regular security updates. The company currently delivers software patches through its Windows Update Web site and through update software in Windows XP, Windows 2000, and Windows Me. The software does not download and install patches by default, but asks a user to select from various options, including simply receiving alerts when an update is available. However, many users continue to ignore the warnings when Microsoft issues a "critical" security update and large numbers of systems fail to get patched. (This was the case with the Blaster worm, which started spreading several weeks after the patch was issued and went on to infect hundreds of thousands of computers.)

The question for Microsoft and its customers is whether patch distribution should be fully automated, so Microsoft can install patches over the Internet without user intervention. Currently, most companies are unwilling to let Microsoft, or any software vendor, have that level of control over their environment. After all, patches can go wrong, creating interoperability issues in seemingly unrelated applications.

However, the benefits of automated patching could also be significant, establishing a more up-to-date and secure PC environment at far less cost to the customer. According to Rob Enderle, principal analyst at Enderle Group in San Jose, "Microsoft has no choice. It has to take patching into its own hands... People really don't want to give Microsoft access, but if they don't, then the patches don't get applied [in a] timely [fashion]. It is about relatives; do folks trust Microsoft more than they trust a hacker?"

How this issue is resolved will ultimately impact how other software vendors manage updates and security patches. It may have an even more far-reaching impact on expectations between software vendors and their customers. At this point, the jury is still out.

Enterprise Call to Action

Software management and currency is a key issue for organizations attempting to reduce costs and improve security for their PC infrastructure. The costs of staying current can be high, yet the risks associated with falling too far behind can also be high. In general, the best strategy is to ensure software management is an active process based on informed analysis. Organizations should:

- Know what software versions are running on their PCs.
- Develop an active approach to determining what changes are on the horizon and the timing of major upgrades.
- Continuously monitor updates, patches, and published vulnerabilities.
- Implement a process for regular PC operating system updates, changes, and security patches.
- Develop a communication plan for employees to increase awareness of the impact of various software updates and the processes surrounding those changes.
- Monitor PC configurations over the network to ensure deployed patches have been properly installed and end users have not made changes that put the network and other users at risk.

Automated tools and a standardized environment are essential to successfully perform these tasks. By actively monitoring and managing their environment, IT functions will have the information and tools they need to make strategic and tactical decisions that benefit their organization.

CHAPTER 7
TOTAL COST OF OWNERSHIP AND FINANCE

Introduction

A strong case can be made for PC management best practices based on cost considerations alone. As shown below, analysts indicate best practices can reduce the total cost of ownership (TCO) for a PC fleet by as much as 30 percent. However, accurately evaluating TCO in an enterprise setting is not simple. A high percentage of total costs are associated with end-user operations, such as self-learning, peer support, and downtime. These costs are difficult to track, yet ignoring them will significantly skew TCO calculations.

One solution is to migrate toward PC management best practices without attempting to measure the specific TCO for your organization. Given the proven benefits of best practices, this may be a reasonable approach in some circumstances, especially in cases where escalating costs are clearly related to a chaotic PC environment. However, the most successful organizations will ultimately implement methodologies for analyzing and tracking TCO in their organization. This can provide valuable insights for planning a migration toward best practices that delivers optimal return on investment (ROI) during each stage, and for building a compelling business case for the required investments.

Over time, the implementation of best practices will provide greater transparency into the PC environment, enabling increasingly accurate measurements of related costs and more accurate ROI assessments for planned operational improvements. As discussed throughout this report, there are many reasons besides TCO for moving toward PC management best practices. However, TCO arguments tend to speak most clearly and universally to business decision makers.

In this chapter, we provide a basic framework for understanding cost categories and life cycle dependencies in a TCO calculation. We also look at some of the key issues with respect to TCO management, including PC refresh rates, automated management tools, purchasing options, and disposal issues.

TCO and the Business Design of PC Practices

To be effective, a TCO model must measure both the direct and indirect costs of owning desktop and notebook computers throughout the PC life cycle. As noted by Thomas Pisello, CEO/president and founder of Alinean, the cost to purchase and deploy new systems is just the tip of the iceberg. Capital costs can be as low as 15 percent of TCO in a typical Windows 2000 environment (Figure 7.1). Operational and administrative costs are significantly higher, and indirect costs, such as end-user training and PC downtime, typically account for well over 50 percent.

Figure 7.1
Windows 2000 TCO by Category

Direct Costs $2,738

Capital: 15%

- Desktops
- Mobile
- Servers
- Printers
- Network

Operations: 25%

- Help Desk
- Technical Services
- Planning and Process

Administration: 3%

- Finance and Administration
- IS Training
- End-user Training

Indirect Costs $3,902

End-user Ops: 32%

- Peer Support
- Self Support
- Data Management
- Formal and Casual Learning

Downtime: 25%

- Planned
- Unplanned

A realistic model of TCO for the PC infrastructure must therefore include the full range of related costs, including support functions such as training, asset management, software updates, backup and recovery solutions, and help desk and onsite technical support. It should also include costs for network and Internet support, printers, security resources (such as authentication and VPN systems and applications, anti-virus protection, etc.), and centralized storage resources.

Within the constraints of practicality, downtime costs should also be tracked and quantified based on IT support costs, lost user productivity, and business process interruptions. There is no single, best way to measure TCO for every organization. Where necessary, industry averages can be used to gain insight into costs that are not readily measurable. Over time, the TCO model can be refined and tied more securely to metrics that can be tracked on an ongoing basis.

Mark Lutchen of PricewaterhouseCoopers recommends mapping processes across the PC life cycle (Figure 7.2). A map of this kind can be valuable for understanding the full complexity of the PC environment.

Appropriate cost and performance metrics should be established for all key functions. Once these relationships are understood and modeled, it becomes possible to track TCO, risk, and value based on specific events, such as a major software upgrade, a surge in hiring, a virus attack, or a large-scale migration to wireless notebooks. The impact of policy and environmental changes can also be modeled, such as a change in standard replacement cycles, an upgrade in help desk services, or the deployment of an automated asset management application. With these tools, administrators can gain vital insights into their specific organization and move toward an optimized PC environment based on a clear understanding of TCO benefits and project ROI.

The Financial Benefits of PC Best Practices

The cost of moving toward PC management best practices is not trivial. Alinean estimates it would cost the average organization $500 to $1,500 per PC to implement best practices in a Microsoft Windows environment (Figure 7.3). If part of that implementation requires an operating system migration, there may be additional costs of about $1,000 per PC. To put these costs into perspective, Alinean estimates the potential annual savings in a well-managed environment at about $1,845 per PC.

Based on this assessment, an average business can expect full payback in about 12 to 18 months. Once payback is achieved, the benefits continue to accrue. There will certainly be ongoing costs to upgrade management tools and processes, but these will be smaller, and the operational and financial transparency of a well-managed PC environment makes it much easier to plan and justify.

Beyond these direct financial considerations, organizations must also consider the impact of best practices on security, compliance, productivity, and agility. In today's legal and regulatory environment, PC fleet management is increasingly essential to limit business risk. It also helps to reduce PC downtime, improve employee performance through regular PC technology refreshes, and enable faster implementation of new applications and business processes.

Figure 7.2
PC Sourcing, Deployment, and Service Example

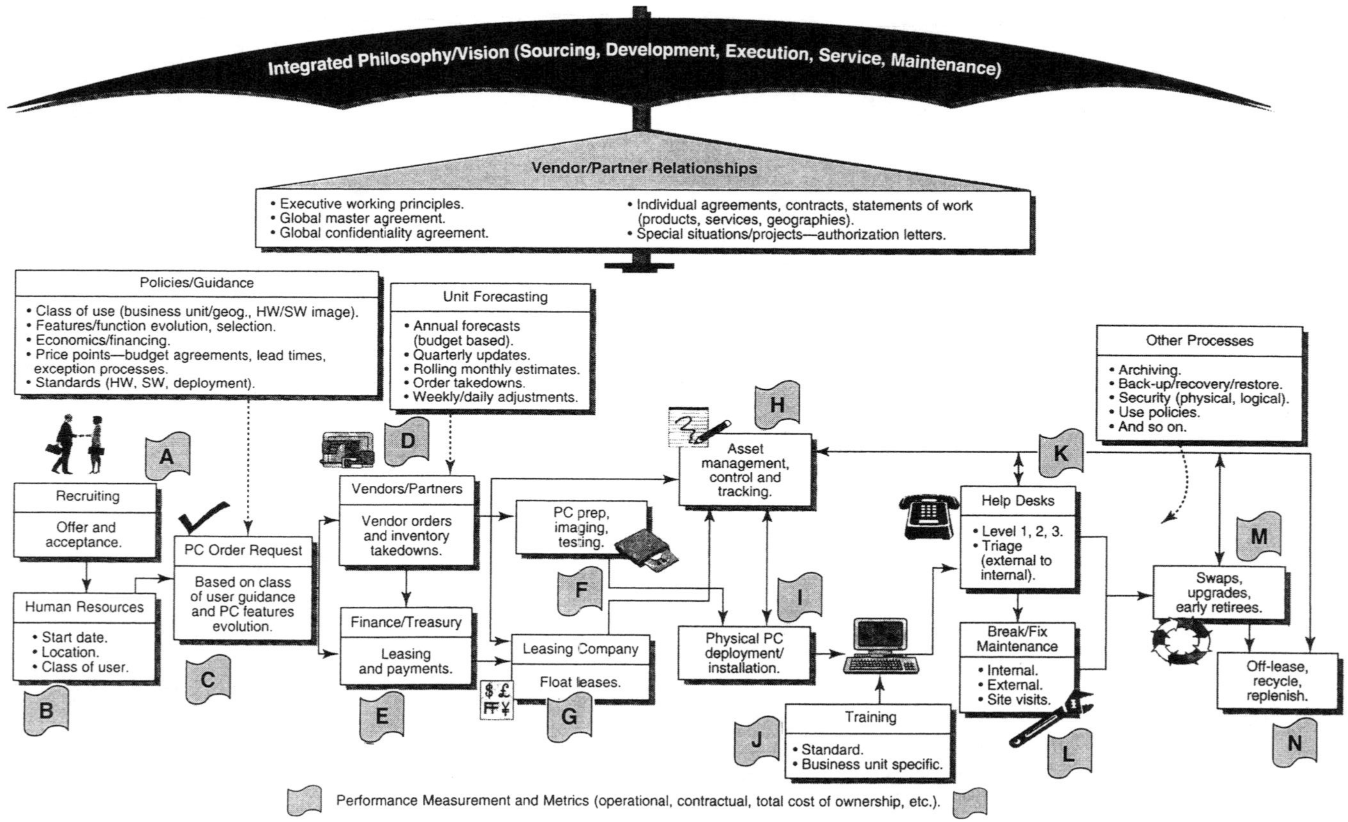

Source: "Managing IT as a Business: A Survival Guide for CEOs," by Mark D. Lutchen, John Wiley & Sons, 2004, p. 173, © 2004 PricewaterhouseCoopers LLP. All rights reserved. "PricewaterhouseCoopers" refers to PricewaterhouseCoopers LLP (a Delaware limited liability partnership) or, as the context requires, other member firms of PricewaterhouseCoopers International Limited, each of which is a separate and independent legal entity.

Figure 7.3
Windows 2000 TCO Drivers

Up to a 26% Savings with Best Practices

$500 to $1,500 per PC to implement
est. savings of $1,845 per PC/year

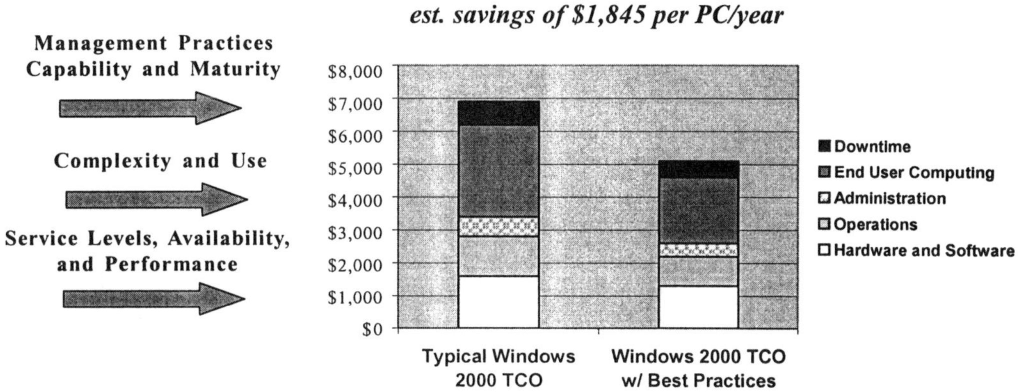

Optimizing PC Replacement Cycles

One of the most valuable aspects of an accurate TCO model is the ability to optimize PC replacement cycles to reduce total costs. For many business decision makers, it seems obvious that PCs should be kept as long as they seem to adequately serve their core function. Yet a closer look reveals it is generally more cost-effective to replace PCs on a regular schedule.

The Cost of PC Maintenance Over Time
Siemens Business Systems (SBS), a provider of PC management outsourcing that supports more than one million PCs, reports that maintenance costs begin to rise after the second year of ownership and the rate of increase accelerates after the third year, which is when warranties typically expire. Based on these factors, SBS recommends a three-year PC replacement cycle for desktops and a two-year cycle for notebooks.

At the July 2003 Technology Audit Forum, keynote speaker Peter Kastner of Aberdeen Group presented research results indicating that only 20 percent to 30 percent of a PC's TCO can be attributed to acquisition and deployment costs.[1] The remaining 70 percent to 80 percent is consumed by operational costs, such as hardware and software maintenance, administration, and help desk support.[2] He also indicated newer PCs have lower ongoing management costs and can appreciably reduce TCO. It is therefore necessary to carefully evaluate total costs when planning the replacement cycle.

The apparent savings of postponing new PC acquisitions must be weighed against the costs and risks of maintaining older PCs. There are three main categories to consider: IT support costs, enterprise security, and employee productivity. All of these factors must be balanced against the costs of acquiring and deploying new PCs, including the costs incurred in disposing of the replaced systems.

Older PCs are more prone to problems and failure than newer machines, as is reflected in the costs for extended warranties. They typically run applications more slowly, and may lack the power to run new or upgraded software. Older systems may also increase enterprise vulnerability to worms, viruses, hackers, and other digital threats, especially if they are running older operating systems and applications. The importance of these variables will of course depend on each company's specific business and IT environment, including their application requirements, the vulnerability of their assets to digital attack, and the quality of their PC management processes. It will also depend on cash flow considerations and PC financing options.

Retaining PCs for longer periods also forces IT organizations to maintain a greater variety of operating systems across the PC fleet. A diverse fleet of PCs and operating systems adds complexity to the costs of maintenance, support, asset management, monitoring, and software updates. Support teams must have higher levels of expertise, and each software upgrade or patch must be tested and deployed differently for each different hardware/software configuration.

Another important cost factor is the decreasing vendor support for older products. Have you noticed that even automobile dealers do not stock parts for vehicles more than five years old? Maintenance can be even more problematic for older PCs. Replacement parts may not be available or the total cost of a repair may equal a significant portion of the replacement cost. In general,

---

[1]Gartner Research (June 2003). For details, see *Linux Desktop TCO: An Overview* (COM-19-8811), Gartner, Inc., June 19, 2003.
[2]For more information on the costs and risks of maintaining older PCs, see the Intel white paper, *The Financial Aspects of PC Fleet Management,* available on the Intel Web site at: www.intel.com/ebusiness/pdf/prod/desktop/pc_fleet_management.pdf

running unsupported hardware and software is not recommended, either from a security or a TCO perspective.

A regular PC refresh cycle offers the additional advantage of improving the consistency of IT spending and operations. Acquisition, deployment, and transition costs are consistent and predictable. Budgets can be planned more effectively, resources can be dedicated to PC transitions, and tools and processes can be optimized on an ongoing basis.

When evaluating TCO to optimize replacement cycles, it is important to pay attention to all factors that impact total costs. For example, a single outage of a network caused by a PC being out of compliance for software support or virus updates can have a significant impact on operational costs, and may impact productivity or revenue. As already discussed, these costs can be difficult to track and are therefore ignored by many businesses. Yet their inclusion can be decisive in accurately understanding TCO and in making a strong case for specific replacement cycle recommendations.

The most important factor in PC security is software currency, especially for the PC operating system (*see Chapter 6*). As long as software versions and security patches are current, older PCs may not present a significantly increased security risk. However, older systems may not provide adequate performance running newer software, or may require significant hardware upgrades to do so. There is also a risk that employees will turn off security features, such as virus scanning or encryption, to accelerate performance on an older PC.

These issues should all be considered when planning PC upgrades. Businesses should also explore the relative costs of software-only upgrades versus complete system replacement. If existing systems provide acceptable performance running the new software, a software-only upgrade may be appropriate. If hardware component upgrades are required (more memory, larger hard drives, etc.), it may be more cost-effective to simply replace the whole system. To the extent possible, IT functions should work to synchronize operating system upgrades and hardware replacement, since it is far more economical to do both together than each separately.

Given the complexity of the issues surrounding PC life cycles, there is no one-size-fits-all solution. Perhaps the most essential point is that companies must look holistically at their PC environment in terms of costs, risk, and value, and manage their replacement schedules accordingly. As evidenced by our research results, overall costs can be reduced by viewing the PC as more than just a commodity and addressing the complete vendor and service relationship as a single equation.

Asset Management

In our survey, many organizations reported a need for improvement in their PC "asset management" and "tracking" processes. Many individuals at the Technology Forum mentioned similar concerns, saying they did not maintain a reliable PC inventory. Because of this, they were unable to perform an adequate TCO analysis or develop a TCO model for driving fleet management decisions.

For IT functions that have not yet deployed network-based management tools, an outsourced assessment service can provide a detailed snapshot of a networked fleet of PCs and provide tools for analyzing the data. This can make it easier to understand TCO issues when planning fleet management strategy or implementing a specific project, such as a large-scale migration. It can also help organizations assess the advantages of deploying an asset management solution.

Today's leading asset management tools track detailed information regarding configurations, software usage, and performance metrics. They can integrate this information with user profiles, physical locations, warranties, and financial information, such as contracts and depreciation. Many solutions also support asset management for non-computing equipment (manufacturing, office equipment, etc.).

Individuals involved in risk management should encourage the enterprise to utilize these types of tools to understand TCO and mitigate risk. Capabilities vary widely, so each organization must evaluate tools and vendors closely with respect to their current requirements and future plans.

Consider the following capabilities in evaluating new tools:

- Ability to perform a real-time inventory over the network. This can help an organization monitor PC security configurations to quickly detect unpatched or misconfigured machines that could compromise enterprise security
- Ability to track diverse assets, including handheld and occasionally connected devices
- Integration with enterprise directories for more efficient policy-based management based on business roles and user profiles
- Ability to drill down quickly to detailed information
- Integration with other processes and applications, such as software distribution and help desk support teams
- Flexible tools for analyzing and presenting data to improve planning and operational efficiency across multiple processes (procurement, deployment, software distribution, etc.)

Automated and Remote PC Management

According to Aberdeen Group, best practices and automated tools for PC management can reduce the annual cost per user by about 50 percent (a typical savings of as much as $4,000 per user). Yet many organizations resist deploying these tools due to the up-front costs as well as the learning curve and process change required to achieve value. It can take several years to move from an unmanaged to a well-managed PC environment, but a carefully planned migration can deliver incremental value along the way. In the process, the PC infrastructure will not only become less costly to maintain, but also more secure and agile as well.

In deploying automated PC management tools, organizations can choose between integrated suites and stand-alone tools that focus on specific management functions. Stand-alone tools may offer better functionality, but integrated suites can help to reduce training costs and leverage benefits across the full PC life cycle.

Because of the advantages of integration, analysts at Giga Information Group now recommend that firms "move to a single management tool for core functions." They say, "Consolidating client management tools and integrating support processes will reduce training costs, infrastructure requirements, and overall support costs by 30 percent or more, and ultimately increase customer (or end-user) satisfaction."[3]

Large enterprises may still benefit from using some best-of-breed tools for specific functions, such as deployment, software migration, patch management, etc. — and may justify the cost of integrating diverse products in-house. However, the value of specific features and functionality should be carefully weighed against the benefits of integrated, off-the-shelf solutions.

Industry Standards

The foundation for automated and remote PC management was laid several years ago when industry leaders and standards organizations began to define and integrate standard technologies for PC platform manageability. Standards adherence is now widespread in platforms intended for enterprise customers, but should still not be taken for granted. A deployed base of systems that adhere to key standards helps to keep your options open as management tools evolve. Consider each of the following:

[3]Giga Research, "Market Overview: Client Systems Management," (RPA-062003-00023), David Friedlander, June 19, 2003.

- **DMI (Desktop Management Interface)** — Provides a standard framework for managing and tracking components in PCs and servers.
- **WfM (Wired for Management)** — Includes essential features for network-based management, including built-in instrumentation, remote wakeup, use of the network as a boot device, and power management capabilities.
- **CIM (Common Information Model)** — A data model for describing overall management information in a network/enterprise environment.
- **WEBEM (Web-based Enterprise Management)** — A set of management and Internet standard technologies developed to unify the management of enterprise computing environments.
- **Other PC Standards** — Standards are continuously evolving for new and emerging technologies. At the time of this research project, support for IEEE 802.X wireless standards (Wi-Fi) is particularly important for all new notebook purchases. Enterprise customers should look for wireless products that support fully ratified 802.X standards and have been validated by the Wi-Fi Alliance. Be wary of PCs and related components that are based on pre-ratified standards. They may be suitable for consumers and small businesses, but are risky for wide-scale enterprise deployment.

PC Disposal

Disposal is a significant and often overlooked episode in the PC life cycle, and it is important to understand the associated costs and risks. The most important issues are security and liability. Sensitive information must be wiped from a PC's hard drive before it is disposed of, stored, or transferred to another user. Data removal should be handled by a knowledgeable technician using controlled procedures to ensure data cannot be recovered. PCs also contain toxic substances and should not be disposed of in public landfills.

For these reasons, it can be useful to outsource PC disposal to a qualified provider. Many PC vendors offer disposal programs. There are also specialty vendors that focus specifically on PC retirement and disposal. Some will pay for systems that can be refurbished and resold, which can improve TCO for PCs that are retired in a timely fashion. Most vendors also work with charitable organizations to ensure the best possible use is made of PCs and notebooks that have outlived their usefulness in an enterprise environment. By either optimizing internal processes or working with a qualified vendor, organizations can improve TCO and mitigate an important source of enterprise risk.

PC Purchasing: Buy or Lease

Buy-versus-lease decisions are typically based more on financial considerations than on technical issues. However, these decisions are also interconnected with planned turnover rates and disposal considerations. The management issues covered elsewhere in this report must also be addressed in a PC buy-versus-lease analysis.

To reduce acquisition and deployment costs for their PCs, some companies now perform reverse auctions in which multiple vendors bid on the price at which they will deliver PCs and/or related services. Management policies and practices will determine whether the reverse auction will apply only to acquisitions or if a company should earn the contract and provide delivery, deployment, and service to standardize support for the entire environment.

Enterprise Call to Action

The value of PC fleet management best practices has been well documented. However, moving toward a standardized and well-managed environment is not easy. The better you understand and document the costs, risks, and value associated with your current environment, the more effectively you can evaluate the real benefits — and justify the costs — of infrastructure and operational upgrades.

The issues are complex and require both technical and financial expertise. For this reason, most organizations would benefit substantially from closer collaboration between their IT and financial professionals. After a number of interviews with finance and purchasing professionals, we found many cases where their expertise had not been utilized in understanding TCO. By bringing both technical and financial expertise to bear on PC management issues, an enterprise can migrate toward best practices and optimized refresh cycles in a controlled fashion that delivers (and documents) better ROI at each step in the process. The value of this collaboration may also extend beyond PC fleet management by establishing tools and processes that can be leveraged across the larger IT environment.

CHAPTER 8
CONCLUSION

This report is a call to action for auditors and management to address the control, security, and efficiency of their networked PC infrastructure. The importance of this infrastructure continues to increase, as core business processes are increasingly leveraged across more users via the corporate network, the Internet, and connected PCs. Administrators also face a growing array of new expectations for performance, mobility, flexibility, and reliability — and a rise in the frequency and severity of digital attacks from the Internet. To top it off, these growing pains coincide with a tough economic climate in which the costs for system upgrades and operational enhancements are under close scrutiny.

These pressures make it all the more essential to closely evaluate the economics of the full PC life cycle, including acquisition, deployment, support, and replacement; to understand the value at risk with respect to the PC infrastructure; and to integrate this evaluation with broader enterprise risk assessments. The best protection and greatest value can be derived only through comprehensive best practices as outlined in this report and summarized below.

Enterprise Action Items

1. Perform a review of the processes used to maintain the PC environment.

2. The networked PC should be managed as an enterprise resource rather than an isolated tool for individual productivity. A review of PC and network management practices should focus first on business control elements (to support Sarbanes-Oxley and other legislated and compliance requirements), and then on asset management and efficiency.

3. Perform a total cost of ownership (TCO) analysis and monitor costs on an ongoing basis. Be sure to include those components not directly related to hardware and software configurations, such as information security, risk management, maintenance, and PC disposal. Factors related to the end user should also be monitored, including user support costs, help desk response time, recovery time frames, risk mitigation, and PC functionality. This is important, since uninformed reductions in technology expenditures can substantially increase end-user related costs, inadvertently driving up enterprise TCO.

4. Determine if standardization and a stable image program is most cost effective. Standardization of the PC environment is a balancing act between diverse user needs, the benefits of uniformity,

and the agility of the enterprise in adapting to new standards. Determine the optimal number of standard images and install efficient processes for implementing regular hardware and software upgrades.

5. Review your risk assessment and perform a gap analysis of insurance coverage for network risk. An enterprise PC risk assessment provides valuable input into the priority of business applications and the degree of risk acceptable to the enterprise. Since insurance coverage for technology and cyber-threats is continually changing, annual review of network risk insurance is warranted.

6. Ensure adequate funding is provided for information security to obtain the optimum return on investment. As described in Chapter 4, the return on security investments can be quantified. This quantification is essential as vulnerabilities and threats continue to increase, and should be a key component of the TCO model. Security is a long-term investment that protects the enterprise from potentially significant loses. The adequacy of security funding must be addressed by executive management and the board of directors, and should be assessed by the internal auditor. Security issues are enterprise-wide concerns and cannot be effectively addressed by individual business units.

7. Develop metrics to improve performance and efficiency.

8. Leverage help desk statistics to determine bottlenecks and operational issues that can further reduce TCO. Statistics on 24/7 PC support, along with detailed failure reports, can help in reducing repetitive failures that increase total costs.

9. Automate business solutions for maintaining the latest operating system software and patches at the PC level. Out-of-compliance PCs should be rapidly identified, taken offline, and remediated. Monitor your network and PC environment so you can detect problems quickly and take immediate action. Standardize, centralize, and automate as much as possible, especially for processes pertaining to software updates and patches.

10. Determine the risk and threat factors in your environment related to old PCs and old operating systems. Old PCs can significantly increase enterprise risk, especially if they are running older operating systems that are no longer supported by the vendor. These old, unsupported configurations should be eliminated from the environment.

11. Continuously improve PC management communication throughout the organization. As noted in the COSO model, a key to success is communication and user education throughout the enterprise. A single out-of-compliance PC can present a vulnerability that poses significant

risk to the enterprise. Every employee must be aware of their responsibility to ensure the computing environment is adequately protected and to report any and all security issues. In addition, management must provide a centralized PC control structure to monitor and manage security patches, virus updates, and safe computing practices. Although many of these functions can be automated, end-user education remains critical in establishing appropriate controls. Company newsletters, the company intranet, PC classes, banner pages, and documented company procedures are all useful for PC "best practices" communication.

12. Determine when to take advantage of new hardware options that allow for improved management, standardization, and redundancy of the networked PC environment.

13. Wireless connectivity can boost productivity and reduce network costs, but is still early in its evolution as an enterprise tool. Security practices and standards tend to closely follow the emergence of new technologies. Each organization must determine the point at which the advantages of deployment outweigh the associated risks and costs of integration.

Jay Stott, Vice President Information Technology Audit for Fidelity Investments, summarizes the following key points:

- Manage PCs as an enterprise resource.
- Determine how to standardize the enterprise PC. If every machine is different, you will need one support person for every five machines. Support people spend all day fixing and patching and trying to figure out what that particular environment is doing. You cannot scale up their service.
- Standardize, centralize, and automate as much as possible that whole process. Centrally deploy updates and patches.
- Protect your data and your operating environment. Hackers really *are* after the data on your machines.
- Monitor your network and PC environment so if something starts to go wrong, you can take immediate action.
- Determine when to take advantage of the newer hardware options that allow for improved management, standardization, and redundancy of the networked PC environment.

APPENDIX A
SURVEY RESULTS

Survey Background

The survey shown below was developed as an early phase of the research project used to prepare this report. The purpose of the survey was to gauge PC activity, current practices, best practices, and areas for improvement. Information from the survey was presented at the Technology Forum sponsored by The IIA Research Foundation on July 24th and 25th, 2003. The survey supported the research purpose of helping to provide concise guidance for management and auditors regarding efficient management and security practices for a fleet of personal computers (PCs).

The survey questions were grouped according to COSO's *Internal Control - Integrated Framework*, and structured to address requirements of the Sarbanes-Oxley Act.

As of July 16, 2003, the survey received 221 responses from participants in the audit, information security, and technology management communities. IIA Japan also posted a copy of this survey, and as of October 29, 2003, had more than 300 responses. A comparison of the results from IIA Japan's survey is included at the end of this appendix. The survey was posted on the GAIN (Global Auditing Information Network) Web site. Invitations to participate in the survey were distributed by The Institute of Internal Auditors, the National Association of Corporate Directors, and the Information Systems Security Association. Other supporting organizations also posted information on their Web sites inviting participation in the survey. Below is a summary of the survey questions and responses:

Control Environment

1. Does your company have information security and acceptable use policies governing the practices and use of PCs?
   ❑ Yes ❑ No ❑ Don't know

   If yes, then answer a, b, c, and d below:

   a. Does this policy include physical security over PCs?
      ❑ Yes ❑ No ❑ Don't Know

   b. Does this policy include logical security over PCs?
      ❑ Yes ❑ No ❑ Don't Know

c. Does this policy include a process to ensure compliance with software license agreements?
❑ Yes ❑ No ❑ Don't Know

d. Does the policy address controls over wireless PCs?
❑ Yes ❑ No ❑ Don't Know

Response: Most had Overall Security Policy for PCs – 93% Yes
a. 73% include physical security over the PC in the policy.
b. 81% include logical security over the PC in the policy.
c. 92% include a process to ensure compliance with software license agreements.
d. Only 30% of the policy/procedure statements for PCs address wireless controls.

2. Does your area assist in making decisions related to the establishment of the criteria, policy, and practices for controlling the PC environment?
❑ Yes ❑ No ❑ Don't Know

Response: Of those answering the survey, 73% of their departments have involvement in establishing policy and procedures related to PCs.

3. Indicate which of the following groups are involved in the design and evaluation of the PC control environment:
❑ Technology Management
❑ Business Management
❑ Information Security
❑ Internal Audit
❑ External Audit
❑ Finance
❑ Risk Management Group
❑ Other (List)

Response: Groups involved in design and evaluation of the PC control environment:
Technology Management (84%)
Information Security (77%)
Internal Audit (58%)
Business Management (33%)
Finance (15%),
Risk Management (14%)
External Audit (14%)
Other (5%)

Risk Assessment

4. Is the overall networked PC environment considered as part of the company-wide risk assessment?
   ❑ Yes ❑ No ❑ Don't Know

Response: Most of the organizations include the networked PC environment in the overall corporate risk assessment – 80%.

5. Are priorities established that differentiate the level of controls required in the PC environment based on the risk assessment?
   ❑ Yes ❑ No ❑ Don't Know

Response: Approximately 50% of the organizations differentiate the level of controls required for the PC environment based on the risk assessment.

6. Has a cost/risk analysis been performed for the enterprise looking at the use of wireless PC communication to provide connectivity to the network?
   ❑ Yes ❑ No ❑ Don't Know

Response: Only 21% have performed a cost analysis for wireless connectivity.

Control Activities

7. Does your organization have enterprise-wide practices for managing controls for the PC environment?
   ❑ Yes ❑ No ❑ Don't Know

If yes, please specify on a scale of 1 to 5, with 5 representing the most tightly enforced standard and 1 being unenforced standards, how you would rate controls over the PC environment?

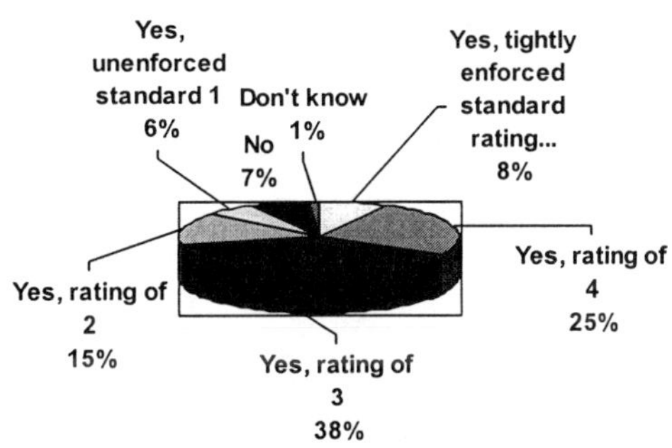

Response: Only 33% of PC environments are considered tightly controlled with a rating of 4 or 5.

8. How often are new virus definition updates moved to individual PCs?
   ❑ Daily ❑ Weekly ❑ Monthly ❑ Quarterly ❑ Yearly

   a. Also, indicate any of the below items that apply:
      ❑ We do not push virus updates to the desktop. It is the responsibility of each individual user.
      ❑ We do not use virus protection software.
      ❑ I don't know how virus protection is handled from an enterprise perspective.

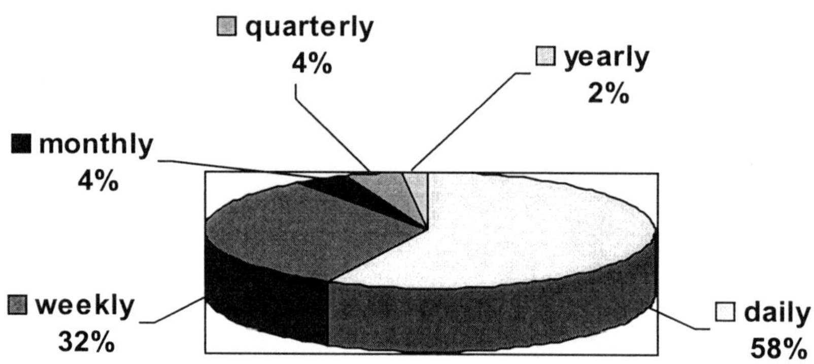

Response: 8% of respondents are responsible for making their own virus updates.
1% did not use virus protection software.
4% did not know how virus protection is handled from an enterprise perspective.

9. Is data from individual PCs backed up on the network automatically to centrally controlled servers?
❑ Yes ❑ No ❑ Don't Know

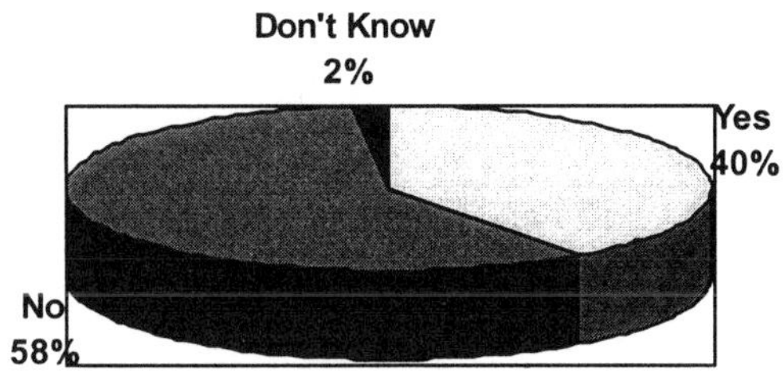

a. Are full image copies of the operating system and various application components backed up automatically to centrally controlled servers?
❑ Yes ❑ No ❑ Don't Know

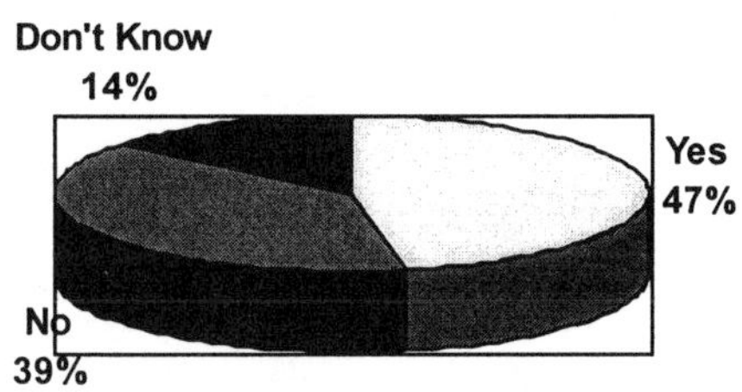

Response: A much higher percentage of PCs had automatic backup of the data than anticipated by the researcher. In addition, the full image restoration at 47% was even more of a surprise. During the Technology Forum the same question was asked and about one-third of the respondents answered Yes on each one.

10. Are software patch updates for various operating systems and other products such as Internet Explorer and Microsoft Office distributed automatically to the desktop?
❑ Yes ❑ No ❑ Don't Know

a. If yes, how often?
❑ Daily ❑ Weekly ❑ Monthly ❑ Quarterly ❑ Yearly
❑ Only as Required ❑ Don't know

Response: 58% of respondents have software patch updates delivered automatically.

Frequency of Automated Software Updates

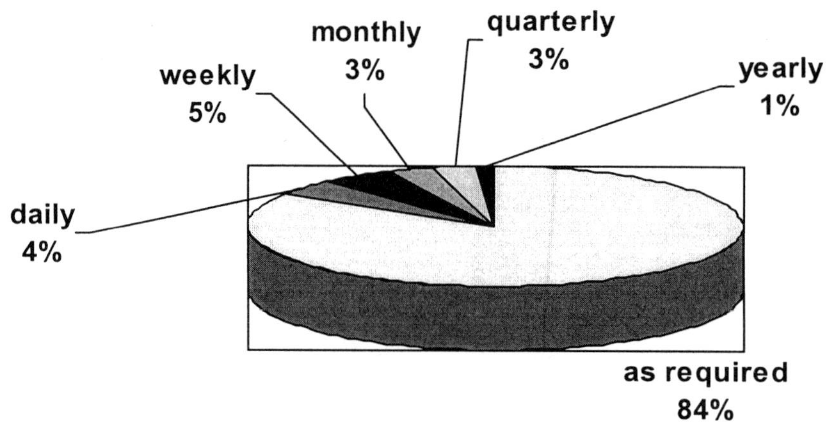

84% of the software patch updates are made as required.

11. Is firewall software a standard on every PC in the environment?

❑ Yes ❑ No ❑ No, Just standard on notebook computers ❑ Don't know

Response: 34% require firewall software on all PCs.
7% require it only on notebook PCs.

12. Are end users (those not involved in PC support) allowed to install various software applications to the PC? (i.e., are end users allowed administrator rights to individual PCs?)
❑ Yes ❑ No ❑ Don't Know

Response: 32% of those responding allow all users administrative rights to install software on PCs.

13. How often does your enterprise upgrade to a new PC operating system?
❑ Annually ❑ Every other year ❑ Every three years
❑ Every four years or greater ❑ Other (please describe) ❑ Don't know

Frequency of Operating System Upgrades

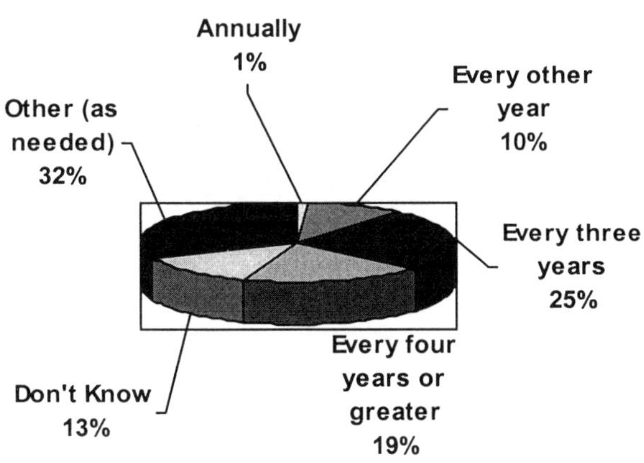

a. Are there criteria for these types of upgrades?
❑ Yes ❑ No ❑ Don't Know

Response: 46% have criteria for operating system upgrades.

b. If yes, what are the criteria? (Please describe.)

Response: Most common answers were cost benefit analysis, functionality, and vendor support.

14. Does your organization ever upgrade the operating system on a PC without also replacing the hardware?
    ❑ Yes ❑ No ❑ Don't Know

Response: 75% will upgrade the operating system without replacing the hardware.

15. How often does your enterprise replace your desktop PC hardware?
    ❑ Annually ❑ Every other year ❑ Every three years
    ❑ Every four years or greater ❑ Don't know

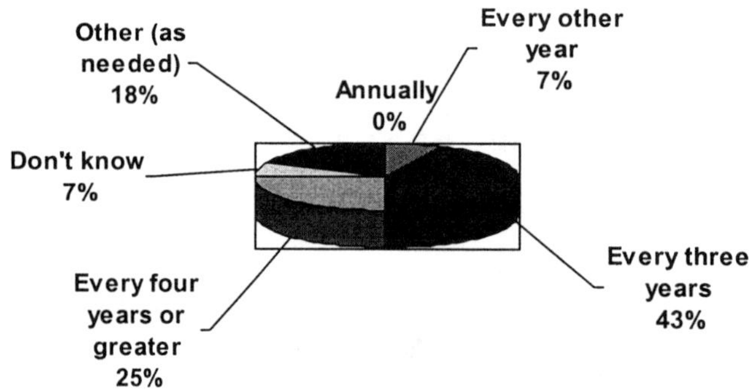

16. How are PCs financed?
    ❑ Purchased ❑ Leased ❑ Both Purchased and Leased

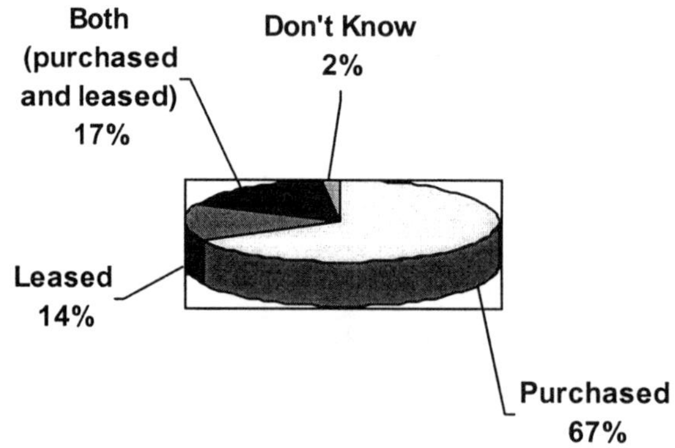

17. How are PCs supported?
    - ❑ Internally within the organization ❑ Support for PCs is outsourced
    - ❑ Both internal support and outsourced

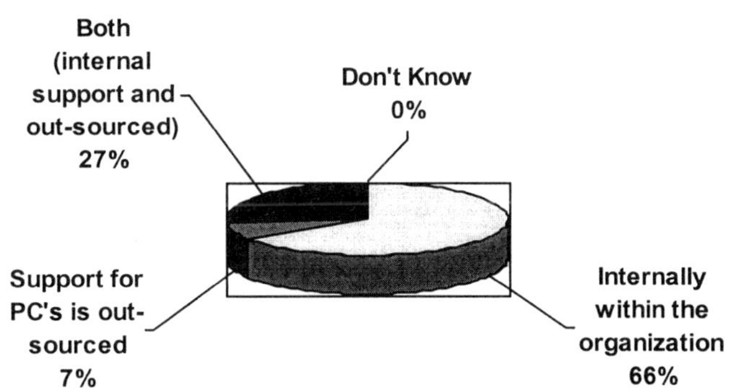

18. Are particular software products prohibited on the desktop (i.e., peer-to-peer information sharing programs, chat programs, games)?
    ❑ Yes ❑ No ❑ Don't Know

If yes, which ones?

Response:

1. **Games – Prohibited by 59%**
2. **Chat – Prohibited by 56%**
3. **Peer-to-Peer File Sharing – Prohibited in 38%, although 18% did not know if it was prohibited**
4. **Music – Prohibited by 38%**

Other mentions:

5. **Prohibit certain Web sites (mentioned a number of times)**
6. **Non-corporate e-mail services**
7. **Non-licensed software and nonbusiness use**

19. Is all data leaving the PC and transmitted through the network encrypted?
    ❑ Yes ❑ No ❑ Don't Know

Response: Only 16% encrypt all data from PC through the network.

20. Is all data encrypted communicated through wireless PCs encrypted?
    ❑ Yes ❑ No ❑ Does not apply to our environment

24% encrypt all data from wireless.
40% stated that encryption for wireless is not applicable.
21% did not know if data from wireless is encrypted.

Information and Communication

21. Are all areas provided company-wide communication either through the intranet or separate mailings on PC controls?
    ❑ Yes ❑ No ❑ Don't Know

Response: 79% have some type of communication related to PC controls distributed throughout the enterprise.

22. Is training provided to business units specifically addressing PC-oriented controls?
    ❑ Yes ❑ No ❑ Don't Know

Response: 44% provide training on PC controls throughout the organization.

Monitoring

23. Which function has the primary responsibility for monitoring the control environment of the networked PC environment?

❑ Internal Audit ❑ Information Technology ❑ Information Security
❑ Line of Business Management ❑ Other (please list)
❑ This type of monitoring does not take place

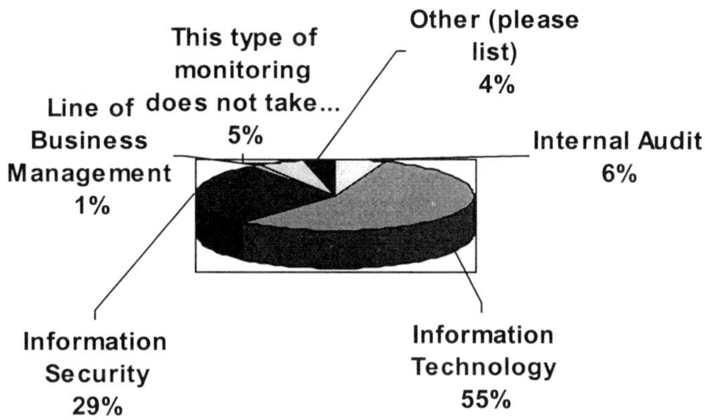

24. Is extensive network monitoring tools in place to monitor PC control compliance?
❑ Yes ❑ No ❑ Don't Know

If yes, do these systems automatically out of compliance conditions?
❑ Yes ❑ No ❑ Don't Know

Response: 45% have extensive network monitoring tools in place to monitor PC control compliance.
48% of those with network monitoring tools in place automatically identify out of compliance conditions.

Other

25. Rate the importance of these control areas within your enterprise.
(On a scale of 1 to 5 with 5 being most important):

___ Existence of standard policies and procedures
___ Enforcement of policies and procedures
___ Migration to standard operating platforms on the PC
___ Life cycle management of the PC
___ Timing of software and hardware upgrades
___ Software patch management of the PC
___ PC inventory management
___ Use of virus protection
___ Use of firewall protection at the PC
___ Disposal of old PC equipment
___ Security management of distributed PC environment
___ Insurance for addressing risk at the PC

RESPONSE: The following areas were ranked as the most important areas in ranked order.

1. **Use of firewall protection at the network infrastructure**
2. **Use of virus protection**
3. **Existence of standard policies and procedures**
4. **Enforcement of policies and procedures**
5. **Security management of distributed PC environment**
6. **Software patch management of the PC**
7. **Use of the firewall protection at the PC**
8. **Migration of standard operating platforms on the PC**
9. **PC inventory management**
10. **Timing of software and hardware upgrades**
11. **Life cycle management of the PC**
12. **Insurance for addressing risk at the PC**
13. **Disposal of old PC equipment**

26. What would be three financial/security best practices your enterprise practices related to the desktop environment? (Open-ended question...)

Most Frequent Responses:

- **Virus protection was the most commonly mentioned best practice (65 responses)**
- **Locked down workstations (18 responses)**
- **Standard images**
- **Security awareness**
- **Frequent software and hardware upgrades**
- **Password controls at the PC**
- **PC inventory controls and asset management**
- **Software license monitoring**
- **Firewalls**

27. In what three ways would you like to see the efficiency or controls improved within your enterprise desktop environment? (Open-ended question...)

Most Frequent Responses:

- **PC asset management**
- **Asset/inventory register cross-referenced to IP database**
- **Security awareness**
- **Automatic backup**
- **Automated compliance monitoring**
- **Automated software license monitoring**
- **Improved intrusion detection**
- **Desktop standardization**
- **Improved enforcement**

28. Most significant factors influencing networked PC control environment (Rate the following on a scale of 1 to 5 with 5 being the most significant factor):

___ Management philosophy on controls
___ Overall management risk assessment
___ The overall control activities in effect in the enterprise
___ The information and communication that goes out to employees
___ The monitoring that is in place to ensure overall compliance
___ In-source or out-source of PC maintenance and help desk
___ Acquisition of the PC: buy versus lease

___ Cost allocation impact on PC fleet management
___ Operating System Used on the PC
___ Others: Please List

RESPONSE: The items below are ranked most significant to least significant.

1. **Management philosophy on controls**
2. **The overall control activities in effect in the enterprise**
3. **The monitoring that is in place to ensure overall compliance**
4. **Overall management risk assessment**
5. **The information and communication that goes out to employees**
6. **In-source or out-source of PC maintenance and help desk**
7. **Cost allocation impact on PC fleet management**
8. **Acquisition of the PC: buy versus lease**
9. **Operating system that is used on the PC**

Demographics

The following questions are related to the demographics of those answering the survey:

29. What is your functional area of responsibility?
    a. Audit
    b. Financial
    c. Information Security
    d. Information Technology
    e. Market Research Analyst
    f. Academic
    g. Other (Please specify.)

Response: Percentages by group:

a. **Audit – 72%**
b. **Financial – 3%**
c. **Information Security – 14%**
d. **Information Technology – 7%**
e. **Market Research Analyst**
f. **Academic**
g. **Other (Please specify) – 4%**

30. Country (Drop-down list)

Responses were international; however, 78% from the U.S. and 7% from Canada.

31. Industry (Drop-down list)

Response: Extremely diverse industries with the top three being:
Financial Services Industry – 20%
Government – 14%
Manufacturing – 11%

32. Number of full-time employees:

Under 500; 501 to 1,000; 1,001 to 5,000; 5,001 to 10,000; 10,001 to 25,000; 25,001 to 50,000; Over 50,000

Response: 72% work for organizations greater than 1,000 employees.
8% work for organizations over 50,000.

33. Are you a member of The Institute of Internal Auditors?
❑ Yes ❑ No

Response: 69% are members of The IIA

Survey Results – Japan

IIA Japan used the survey developed for this research project to determine specific areas of difference in the responses for the Japan environment. We would like to thank Kyoko Shimizu, Manager of Technology and Security Risk Service of Shin Nihon & Company, for leading those efforts and summarizing the data. The survey responses for over 300 were within 15 percent of the responses in the overall survey, except for those differences described below.

Established Practices	Japan	Overall
Have processes in place to ensure compliance with software license agreements.	74%	92%
Differentiate the level of controls required for the PC environment based on risk.	29%	50%
Have performed a cost analysis for wireless connectivity.	65%	21%
Update virus definitions daily.	87%	58%
Back up PC data daily.	14%	40%
Perform full image backups.	22%	47%
Perform automatic software patch management daily.	23%	4%
Require firewall software on every PC in the environment.	61%	34%
Replace desktop PCs every three years.	13%	43%
Replace desktop PCs every four years.	41%	25%
Have criteria for operating system upgrades.	25%	46%
Will upgrade operating systems without replacing hardware.	52%	75%
Upgrade operating systems every four years.	64%	19%
Upgrade operating systems on an as-needed basis.	11%	32%
Purchase rather than lease equipment.	24%	67%
Have extensive network monitoring tools in place to monitor PC control compliance.	25%	45 %
Employ best practices in asset management.	High	Low
Employ best practices in using standard PC images.	Low	High
Improvements needed in security awareness	High	Low

The survey used in this research can also be used by other IIA chapters, National Institutes, or countries and performed online using the GAIN Flash Survey process similar to the overall survey. Individual IIA affiliates can work with IIA Global Headquarters to have the survey translated, linked from the individual country site, and have the results summarized. This data can then be compared to the survey data contained in this Appendix for analysis and would also be available online. Contact Don Sparks, Assistant Vice President of Online Services, at dsparks@theiia.org to coordinate.

APPENDIX B
TECHNOLOGY AUDIT FORUM

Introduction

The third phase of this project was a Technology Audit Forum held July 24th and July 25th in Orlando, Florida. The forum was designed to address key issues for this report with two major roundtable discussions focused on "Total Cost of Ownership" and "Information Security." The input from the forum has been integrated throughout this report. Participants were involved in extensive discussions on key topics, including business risk, insurance, regulatory issues (including Sarbanes-Oxley), audit approaches, PC costs, and information security. Speakers at the forum included chief audit executives and chief information officers, as well as subject matter experts in a variety of key areas, including audit, technology, finance, and consulting.

Agenda

Thursday, July 24

8:30 a.m.	Forum Kickoff William G. Bishop, III, President, The IIA Mark Salamasick, Research Project Leader Susan Watson, VP, CXO Media Services, Moderator
8:45 a.m.	Keynote: *Future Trends of the PC Networked Environment* Peter Kastner, EVP and Chief Research Officer, Aberdeen Group
9:30 a.m.	*Summary of Research Survey Results and Discussion of Project Objectives* Mark Salamasick, Research Project Leader
10:30 a.m.	*Insurance Industry Best Practices to Risk Mitigation* Tim Burke, Aon Kurt Suhs, NetDiligence
1:00 p.m.	*A Chief Audit Executive's View of Audit's Role* Jay Stott, Vice President, Information Technology Audits, Fidelity
2:00 p.m.	*Return on Information Security Investment* Jeff Curtis, Ernst & Young
3:30 p.m.	*The Total Cost of Ownership of the Desktop* (Facilitated Panel Discussion) Peter Kastner, EVP & Chief Research Officer, Aberdeen Group (moderator) Suzanne Hopgood, President & CEO, The Hopgood Group, LLC Mark Lutchen, Partner, PricewaterhouseCoopers

Tom Pisello, CEO/President and Founder, Alinean
Tom Stewart, Manager, IT Strategic Finance, Intel Corporation

7:00 p.m. *Audit Committee Perspectives on Information Reliability, Security, and Assurance*
Suzanne Hopgood, President & CEO, The Hopgood Group, LLC

Friday, July 25

8:30 a.m. *The Impact of Sarbanes-Oxley on the Technology Environment*
Tripp Davis, PricewaterhouseCoopers

10:00 a.m. *Focus on Security in a Distributed Environment* (Facilitated Panel Discussion)
Susan Watson, Moderator and CXO Media
Jeff Curtis, E&Y
Tripp Davis, PricewaterhouseCoopers
Kim Walker, JP Morgan
Steve Skibinski, Intel

11:45 a.m. *Forum Wrap-up, Conclusions, and Next Steps*
Mark Salamasick, Research Project Leader

12:00 p.m. Forum Conclusion

APPENDIX C
KEY GUIDANCE, REFERENCES, AND ARTICLES

Many articles and references were beneficial in this research. They spanned a broad range of topics, including new and emerging hardware and software technologies, effective management practices, information security, business continuity and recovery, intrusion protection and event handling, risk management, financial practices, and much more. If fact, there is much more information available relevant to PC management practices than could reasonably be included in one report. This report, therefore, represents a distillation of meaningful information into a manageable format. Perhaps someday someone will write an encyclopedia of PC management practices. Until then, here are some concepts and references you may find useful.

Privacy

There have been numerous privacy debacles in recent years, and many of them relate specifically to PC management practices. Others are more relevant to Web-site management and the use of PCs in accessing Web sites. The following list summarizes the lessons learned from those events. It also offers some recommendations that are particularly suitable for organizations that are just starting to address privacy issues or develop related policy. The examples used to illustrate key points have been cited in the popular and technical press.

- **Say What You Do and Do What You Say** — Ensure that all privacy policy statements posted on a Web site are supported by actual practices. Conduct periodic reviews of policies and practices to ensure that practices comply with policies and are consistent across business units. For larger organizations, this may mean developing an internal privacy compliance process. In the absence of privacy laws and regulations, the U.S. Federal Trade Commission has brought actions under deceptive trade practices laws. This is also applicable to liquidations of assets in bankruptcy or when organizations or their assets are bought and sold. In summer 2001, concerns were raised about the bankruptcy of Egghead.com and their consumer lists.

- **Do the Right Thing** — It may sound trite or altruistic, but it really is smart business to do what is right or ethical in regard to privacy, as opposed to what is legally permissible. Numerous privacy issues have been tried in the court of public opinion where the penalty is loss of trust and possible activist reaction. Although perhaps not illegal, tracking individual activities (such as clicking on ads) can result in an extremely negative public reaction.

- **Patch Security Holes in Operating Systems** — A number of issues arise because vendors of well-known computing platforms release their operating systems with inherent security weaknesses. Additionally, organizations fail to apply the patches to the security holes as quickly as hackers exploit them. Proactively monitor your operating system supplier by signing up with their automatic notification processes for any known security weaknesses and associated fixes. When the Code Red worm was active in August 2001, the operating system patches required had been widely available for months, and the industry press was full of warnings, yet hundreds of thousands of machines were compromised because they were not updated.

- **Prevent Exposed E-mail Lists** — When sending e-mail to user lists, individuals and businesses frequently compromise privacy by inadvertently exposing the full mailing list to all addressees. Use standard agents to generate mailing lists and test to make sure that the software blind copies all recipients instead of printing out their full e-mail addresses.

- **Examine URL Contents** — Some Web sites redirect users to affiliated sites and include personal identifying information (PII) in the URL. Examine all links external to the Web site and use a packet sniffer to ensure the URL contents do not contain PII, especially if this is not disclosed in the privacy policy.

- **Avoid PC/User ID Tags that Can Track Machines/Users** — A number of organizations have raised the hackles of consumer privacy advocates by tagging software registration wizards or online transactions with a unique ID, including a GUID Processor Serial Number, or other identifying numbers that can be used to profile a user. Use a packet sniffer to ensure an ID tag is not being sent to a Web site.

- **Avoid Web Bugs or at Least Disclose Their Use** — While cookies can be managed by the browser or cookie management products, Web bugs, 1x1 pixel objects loaded from a third-party Web site, profile a user in such a way that they are unaware and cannot opt out. Examine the source of Web pages for 1x1 pixel objects loaded from a third-party Web site. (Not familiar with Web Bugs? Search www.ITAudit.org for explanatory information.)

- **Avoid Software that "Phones Home"** — Software vendors sometimes engineer products to automatically send information back to the manufacturer. Test the registration procedures of all purchased software diligently, including what is captured in cookies and URLs. Examine software offline to determine if agents are active that can sense an Internet connection or attempt to place the computer in online mode. Inventory all software on the Web site and ensure any data transferred off the Web site is disclosed.

- **Provide Choice** — Many privacy issues have resulted from failure to provide meaningful choices that put individuals in control of their information. The general rule is not to use PII for any secondary purposes unless the individual has been provided a choice as to how that information will be managed on their behalf.

- **Cleanse Demonstration Software** — Development teams often take a cut of a live customer database to use as test data or demo data when demonstrating to potential customers that new applications reflect reality. It is standard practice in most organizations, whether it is an official procedure or not. At a minimum, however, data and software quality assurance testing must include a checkpoint to remove live data, even if it is only used internally.

- **Test Third-party Software for Glitches** — Follow the manual and test thoroughly. Don't assume installations from shrink-wrap are preset with the right options. As one example, incorrectly installed shopping cart software has been known to reveal customer names, addresses, and account numbers in response to certain keyword searches.

- **Protect PII Even More Diligently When Change is Occurring** — When making major changes on your Web site it is important to keep traditional security and firewalls, as well as content management processes, active until the final transition. A Web site made news by exposing employee e-mail accounts and encrypted passwords during domain name migration.

- **Confirm Employees Understand Privacy Policy** — Training and awareness of good privacy practices and policy is critical to ensuring compliance. Programs should include training for new hires, FAQs, and regular updates to prevent inappropriate social engineering and inadvertent disclosure of personal data. In one case, a customer service technician revealed customer account information to an outside party despite policy restrictions against disclosing such data.

- **Appoint a Chief Privacy Officer** — Even if this is not a full-time position, responsibility for privacy policy compliance should be assigned to an executive of the organization. Ensure the function is adequately funded, sufficiently influential to drive change, and supported by the highest levels of the organization.

Index of Reference Material

TITLE	URL LINKS	SOURCE	AUTHOR(S)	Date
2003 Global Security Survey	http://www.deloitte.com/dtt/cda/doc/content/Global%20Security%20Survey%202003.pdf	Deloitte Touche Tohmatsu	R. Power O. Curst	2003
Additional Areas for Risk Management to be Concerned About	http://www.theiia.org/itaudit/index.cfm?fuseaction=forum&fid=271	The Institute of Internal Auditors	D. Hall	Apr. 2001
Are You Checking for the Trojan?	http://www.theiia.org/itaudit/index.cfm?fuseaction=forum&fid=329	The Institute of Internal Auditors	D. Hall	Aug. 2001
Basic Computer Security	http://www.theiia.org/itaudit/index.cfm?fuseaction=forum&fid=225	The Institute of Internal Auditors	D. Hall	Dec. 2000
Beyond Viruses	http://www.theiia.org/itaudit/index.cfm?fuseaction=forum&fid=401	The Institute of Internal Auditors	D. Stang	Jan. 2002
Coping with RATS	http://www.theiia.org/itaudit/index.cfm?fuseaction=forum&fid=405	The Institute of Internal Auditors	D. Stang	Feb. 2002
Digital Leakage: A Crisis of Confidentiality	http://www.theiia.org/itaudit/index.cfm?fuseaction=forum&fid=487	The Institute of Internal Auditors	M. Lambert	Sept. 2002
ESAC Managing Computer Resources–Technical Overview	http://www.theiia.org/itaudit/index.cfm?fuseaction=forum&fid=496	The Institute of Internal Auditors	B. Sannerud J. Silltow	Oct. 2002
Finding the Electronic Evidence	http://www.theiia.org/itaudit/index.cfm?fuseaction=forum&fid=461	The Institute of Internal Auditors	M. Grossman	Jul. 2002
Forensic Auditing	http://www.theiia.org/itaudit/index.cfm?fuseaction=forum&fid=108	The Institute of Internal Auditors	A. Sheldon	Jan. 1999
Hostile Applets	http://www.theiia.org/itaudit/index.cfm?fuseaction=forum&fid=180	The Institute of Internal Auditors	K. Foggon	Aug. 1999
Information Security Impacting Securities Valuations	http://www.theiia.org/itaudit/index.cfm?fuseaction=forum&fid=143	The Institute of Internal Auditors	M. Acuff	Aug. 2000
The Internet: It's Full of Holes	http://www.theiia.org/itaudit/index.cfm?fuseaction=forum&fid=378	The Institute of Internal Auditors	D. Hall	Apr. 2001

TITLE	URL LINKS	SOURCE	AUTHOR(S)	Date
Internet Security Software: The Ultimate Internet Infrastructure - Part 1	http://www.theiia.org/itaudit/index.cfm?fuseaction=forum&fid=145	The Institute of Internal Auditors	C. Jones	Feb. 2001
Internet Security Software: The Ultimate Internet Infrastructure - Part 2	http://www.theiia.org/itaudit/index.cfm?fuseaction=forum&fid=146	The Institute of Internal Auditors	C. Jones	Mar. 2001
Internet Security Software: The Ultimate Internet Infrastructure - Part 3	http://www.theiia.org/itaudit/index.cfm?fuseaction=forum&fid=147	The Institute of Internal Auditors	C. Jones	Apr. 2001
Internet Security Software: The Ultimate Internet Infrastructure - Part 8	http://www.theiia.org/itaudit/index.cfm?fuseaction=forum&fid=152	The Institute of Internal Auditors	C. Jones	Aug. 2001
Internet Security Software: The Ultimate Internet Infrastructure, Part 12	http://www.theiia.org/itaudit/index.cfm?fuseaction=forum&fid=337	The Institute of Internal Auditors	C. Jones	Oct. 2001
Internet Security Software: The Ultimate Internet Infrastructure, Part 13	http://www.theiia.org/itaudit/index.cfm?fuseaction=forum&fid=340	The Institute of Internal Auditors	C. Jones	Oct. 2001
IT Auditing Without Pain – Part 12 – Intellectual Property Rights	http://www.theiia.org/itaudit/index.cfm?fuseaction=forum&fid=450	The Institute of Internal Auditors	A. Oliphant	June 2002
Liability for You if You've Been Hacked	http://www.theiia.org/itaudit/index.cfm?fuseaction=forum&fid=103	The Institute of Internal Auditors	M. Grossman	Aug. 2000
Managing Desktop Security in an Insecure Environment	http://www.theiia.org/itaudit/index.cfm?fuseaction=forum&fid=5422	The Institute of Internal Auditors	M. Salamasick C. Le Grand	July 2003
Network Computing and Control - Part 1	http://www.theiia.org/itaudit/index.cfm?fuseaction=forum&fid=184	The Institute of Internal Auditors	D. Gilliam	July 2000
Network Computing and Control - Part 2	http://www.theiia.org/itaudit/index.cfm?fuseaction=forum&fid=185	The Institute of Internal Auditors	D. Gilliam	July 2000
Network Computing and Control - Part 3	http://www.theiia.org/itaudit/index.cfm?fuseaction=forum&fid=186	The Institute of Internal Auditors	D. Gilliam	Sept. 2000
New Areas for Your Risk Management Program	http://www.theiia.org/itaudit/index.cfm?fuseaction=forum&fid=269	The Institute of Internal Auditors	D. Hall	Mar. 2001

Title	URL Links	Source	Author(s)	Date
News: September, 2002- Articles on Laptop Security, Wireless Security, and OS Security	http://www.theiia.org/itaudit /index.cfm?fuseaction=forum &fid=485	The Institute of Internal Auditors	T. McCollum	Sept. 2002
PC Market Show Signs of Recovery	http://www.informationweek .com/story/showArticle.jhtml ?articleID=9901359	TechWeb News	A. Gonsalves	May 2003
The President's Commission on Critical Infrastructure Protection and Information Security – Part 1	http://www.theiia.org/itaudit /index.cfm?fuseaction=forum &fid=117	The Institute of Internal Auditors	W. Ozier	Nov. 1998
Protecting Against Wireless Threats	http://www.theiia.org/itaudit /index.cfm?fuseaction=forum &fid=5426	The Institute of Internal Auditors	M. Attaway	July 2003
Security Basics: A White Paper	http://www.theiia.org/itaudit /index.cfm?fuseaction=forum &fid=212	The Institute of Internal Auditors	T. Feinman D. Goldman R. Wong N. Cooper	Jun. 1999
Software-compliance Audits Reduce Piracy Exposure	http://www.theiia.org/itaudit /index.cfm?fuseaction=forum &fid=524	The Institute of Internal Auditors	R. Harmer	Jan. 2003
Software Management, Part 4: Ordering	http://www.theiia.org/itaudit /index.cfm?fuseaction=forum &fid=251	The Institute of Internal Auditors	J. Silltow	Feb. 2000
Software Management, Part 7: Installation	http://www.theiia.org/itaudit /index.cfm?fuseaction=forum &fid=254	The Institute of Internal Auditors	J. Silltow	July 2000
Systems Security: It's More Important Than Ever	http://www.theiia.org/itaudit /index.cfm?fuseaction=forum &fid=220	The Institute of Internal Auditors	A. Holzinger	May 2000
Upgrading to Windows 2000	http://www.theiia.org/itaudit /index.cfm?fuseaction=forum &fid=131	The Institute of Internal Auditors	R. Harmer	Jan. 2001
What Auditors Should Know About E-appliances	http://www.theiia.org/itaudit /index.cfm?fuseaction=forum &fid=81	The Institute of Internal Auditors	J. Yu	Apr. 2000

APPENDIX D
A TEMPLATE FOR DOCUMENTATION AND COMPLIANCE- SARBANES-OXLEY IMPACT ON TECHNOLOGY

As we developed material for this project and discussed the models being used for compliance with regulatory issues, we found many internal audit groups using the COSO framework for compliance with Sarbanes-Oxley.

In 1992, the Committee of Sponsoring Organizations of the Treadway Commission (COSO) developed a model for evaluating internal controls. This model has been adopted as the generally accepted framework for internal control and is widely recognized as the definitive standard against which organizations measure the effectiveness of their systems. The COSO model defines internal control as "a process, effected by an entity's board of directors, management and other personnel, designed to provide reasonable assurance of the achievement of objectives in the following categories:

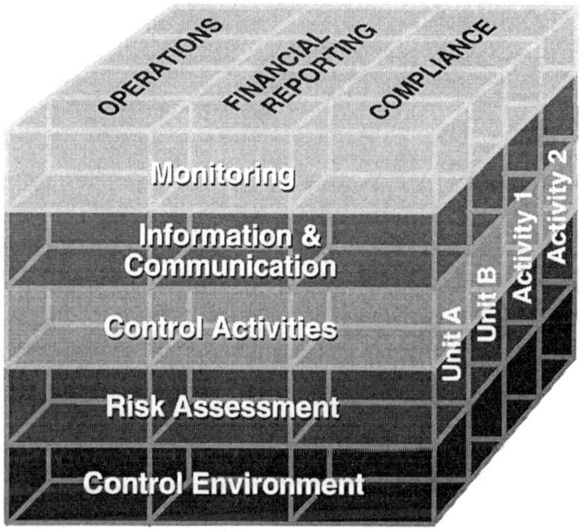

- Effectiveness and efficiency of operations.
- Reliability of financial reporting.
- Compliance with applicable laws and regulations."

In an "effective" internal control system, the five components work to support the achievement of an entity's mission, strategies, and related business objectives, including:

- *Control Environment*
  - Integrity and Ethical Values
  - Commitment to Competence

  - Board of Directors and Audit Committee
  - Management's Philosophy and Operating Style
  - Organizational Structure
  - Assignment of Authority and Responsibility
  - Human Resource Policies and Procedures
- *Risk Assessment*
  - Company-wide Objectives
  - Process-level Objectives
  - Risk Identification and Analysis
  - Managing Change
- *Control Activities*
  - Policies and Procedures
  - Security (Application and Network)
  - Application Change Management
  - Business Continuity/Backups
  - Outsourcing
- *Information and Communication*
  - Quality of Information
  - Effectiveness of Communication
- *Monitoring*
  - Ongoing Monitoring
  - Separate Evaluations
  - Reporting Deficiencies

The following template provides an example of how the COSO model can be used as a framework for the processes related to managing the PC control environment. The information is intended for illustrative purposes only, and should be customized to your own environment. The authors would suggest that PC functions determined to be critical to the financial reporting aspects of the organization should be documented and tested as part of management oversight for regulatory purposes.

Major Exposure: Financial Reporting/Asset Management

Control Environment:
Inadequacy of PC equipment inventories and the reporting of owned assets.

Lack of accountability for contractual agreements between the company and outside PC support vendors.

Control Activities:
Ongoing contract performance tracking and reporting to ensure contract goals are being achieved.

PC equipment inventories are tracked to ensure software compliance, security patches, and software maintenance.

Information & Communication
Monthly and quarterly detailed reporting on capital expenditure and general expenses (salary, travel, telecom expenses, supplies, etc.).

Detailed reports as needed to adjust budgets to account for organizational changes and consolidations.

Management Monitoring:
Weekly status meetings to discuss issues.

Ongoing management accountability for budget spending.

Major Exposure: Operational (Including safeguarding of assets)

Control Environment:
Dependency on vendors for PC equipment and support.

Lack of robust contingency plans to support functional operations.

Policies and procedures not consistent with management's objectives and goals.

Lack of skilled resources necessary to support the rapid deployment of new technology.

Challenge of merging various non-homogeneous and diverse environments into a consistent, seamless delivery of PC services.

Control Activities:
Implementation of a robust "layered" approach to architecture design to provide redundancy and reliability.

Scheduled tests of PC recoverability through disaster recovery exercises.

24x7x365 monitoring from nationwide network command centers which provide problem identification and escalation

Ongoing projects to develop and implement consistent practices.

Information & Communication:
Distribution of management policy and procedures to line units via the Intranet, team meetings, and company newsletter.

Personnel attend various industry seminars to stay abreast of emerging issues and technologies in order to adequately support delivery of services to the PC.

Management Monitoring:
Weekly status meetings to discuss issues.

Ongoing management review of capacity reports, significant event reports, and client feedback.

Major Exposure: PC Project Management Implementation

Control Environment:
Inadequate communication between project and process personnel that delays or substantially inhibits the ongoing maintenance and support of PC computing systems.

Project selection of a technology platform that is inconsistent with strategic technology objectives and/or fails to meet the technical architecture requirements.

Incorrect management decisions resulting from over or understated project costs or incomplete economic evaluations.

The success of a project may be jeopardized by the following:
- Lack of involvement by the business.
- Lack of effectiveness in communicating the project methodology to participating parties.
- Inappropriate staffing of the project team.

Control Activities:
The Centralized PC Support Group has responsibility for coordinating the integration of new microcomputer equipment and technology.

Centralized project support tracks all projects for the various lines of business and represents information technology at all project meetings.

Management has a process in place to coordinate and manage the implementation of PC technology as part of larger projects. Some components of this process include:

- Preparation of a requirements analysis by the end user.
- Compliance with hardware and software supported products listing.
- Automated tracking of network hardware through the phases of implementation (i.e., future, integration, turnover, production).
- Requiring a client acceptance document before production implementation.

Centralized Technology Group works closely with the supported products and advises lines of business and various other ongoing projects to ensure that requested hardware and software is consistent with strategic technology goals and objectives and technical architecture.

Information & Communication:
The various projects throughout the organization are coordinated by the various lines of business management and they conduct regular meetings to communicate status of projects to upper management.

Centralized PC Support Group works closely with the projects group to stay abreast of potential projects affecting the enterprise PC network.

Standards and procedures relating to PC hardware and software are communicated through the publication of the supported products listing for microcomputer equipment.

Management Monitoring:
The Centralized Project Support Group works closely with the various lines of business to stay abreast of potential projects affecting information technology platforms including the intranet. The Centralized Network Group also communicates with the Centralized Supported Products Evaluation Committee to ensure that projects involving the purchase of new microcomputer hardware are consistent with the overall technology strategy.

Exposure:
Major Exposure: Regulatory

Exposure Environment:
Noncompliance with:
Sarbanes-Oxley
BS 7799
HIPAA
Gramm-Leach-Bliley

Control Activities:
Implementation of consistent, reliable technology platforms having standard tools and practices for security and data administration.

Thorough testing and certification of products within the technology environment to ensure compliance with regulations and software management standards.

Engineering design and implementation based on business requirements, managing projects from inception to full implementation, and serving as the primary point of entry for projects.

Periodic testing of contingency plans to ensure recoverability of systems and applications.

Delivery of Web-enabled applications through the development of a secured firewall complex.

Information & Communication:
Information security has developed a standards guide for all employees related to information protection and awareness. It is currently available on their intranet site and is also available in hard copy for distribution.

Management Monitoring:
Extensive integration and packing requirements are communicated to ensure standardization and consistency.

Architectural guidelines are communicated through the architectural standards committee.

APPENDIX E RECOMMENDED STANDARDS AND BEST PRACTICES

CERT/CC Recommended Practices

The chart below provides recommendations on configuring the workstation environment and is considered by CERT as best practice. The CERT® Coordination Center (CERT/CC) is a center of Internet security expertise located at the Software Engineering Institute, a federally funded research and development center operated at Carnegie Mellon University.

Area	Recommended Practice/Reference
Planning deployment	1. Develop a computer deployment plan that includes security issueswww.cert.org/security-improvement/practices/p065.html
Configuring workstations	2. Keep operating systems and applications software up to date www.cert.org/security-improvement/practices/p067.html 3. Configure computers for user authenticationwww.cert.org/security-improvement/practices/p069.html 4. Configure computer operating systems with appropriate object, device, and file access controlswww.cert.org/security-improvement/practices/p070.html 5. Identify data that characterize systems and aid in detecting signs of suspicious behaviorwww.cert.org/security-improvement/practices/p091.html 6. Manage logging and other data collection mechanismswww.cert.org/security-improvement/practices/p092.html 7. Configure computers for file backupswww.cert.org/security-improvement/practices/p071.html 8. Protect computers from viruses and similar programmed threats www.cert.org/security-improvement/practices/p072.html 9. Configure computers for secure remote administrationwww.cert.org/security-improvement/practices/p073.html 10. Configure computers to provide only selected network services www.cert.org/security-improvement/practices/p038.html

Area	Recommended Practice/Reference
	11. Configure network service clients to enhance securitywww.cert. org/security-improvement/practices/p030.html 12. Configure multiple computers using a tested model configuration and a secure replication procedure www.cert.org/security-improvement/practices/p036.html
Maintaining work-station integrity	13. Allow only appropriate physical access to computers www.cert.org/security-improvement/practices/p074.html
Improving user awareness	14. Develop and promulgate an acceptable use policy for workstations www.cert.org/security-improvement/practices/p034.html

PC Security Tips – Provided by the National Cyber Security Alliance:

1. **Use protection software "*anti-virus software*" and keep it up to date.**
Make sure you have anti-virus software on your computer! Anti-virus software is designed to protect you and your computer against known viruses so you don't have to worry. But with new viruses emerging daily, anti-virus programs need regular updates, like annual flu shots, to recognize these new viruses. Be sure to update your anti-virus software regularly! The more often you keep it updated, say once a week, the better. Check with the Web site of your anti-virus software company to see some sample descriptions of viruses and to get regular updates for your software. Stop viruses in their tracks!

2. **Don't open e-mail from unknown sources.**
A simple rule of thumb is that if you don't know the person who is sending you an e-mail, be very careful about opening the e-mail and any file attached to it. Should you receive a suspicious e-mail, the best thing to do is to delete the entire message, including any attachment. Even if you do know the person sending you the e-mail, you should exercise caution if the message is strange and unexpected, particularly if it contains unusual hyperlinks. Your friend may have accidentally sent you a virus. Such was the case with the "I Love You" virus that spread to millions of people in 2001. When in doubt, delete!

3. **Use hard-to-guess passwords.**
Passwords will only keep outsiders out if they are difficult to guess! Don't share your password, and don't use the same password in more than one place. If someone should happen to guess one of your passwords, you don't want them to be able to use it in other places. The golden

rules of passwords are: (1) A password should have a minimum of eight characters, be as meaningless as possible, and use uppercase letters, lowercase letters, and numbers, e.g., xk28LP97; (2) change passwords regularly, at least every 90 days; (3) do not give out your password to anyone!

4. **Protect your computer from Internet intruders — use "*firewalls*."**
   Equip your computer with a firewall! Firewalls create a protective wall between your computer and the outside world. They come in two forms — software firewalls that run on your personal computer, and hardware firewalls that protect a number of computers at the same time. They work by filtering out unauthorized or potentially dangerous types of data from the Internet, while still allowing other (good) data to reach your computer. Firewalls also ensure that unauthorized persons can't gain access to your computer while you're connected to the Internet. You can find firewall hardware and software at most computer stores nationwide. Don't let intruders in!

5. **Don't share access to your computers with strangers. Learn about file-sharing risks.**
   Your computer operating system may allow other computers on a network, including the Internet, to access the hard drive of your computer in order to "share files." This ability to share files can be used to infect your computer with a virus or look at the files on your computer if you don't pay close attention. So unless you really need this ability, make sure you turn off file sharing. Check your operating system and your other program help files to learn how to disable file sharing. Don't share access to your computer with strangers!

6. **Disconnect from the Internet when not in use.**
   Remember that the digital highway is a two-way road. You send and receive information on it. Disconnecting your computer from the Internet when you're not online lessens the chance that someone will be able to access your computer. And if you haven't kept your anti-virus software up to date, or don't have a firewall in place, someone could infect your computer or use it to harm someone else on the Internet. Be safe and disconnect!

7. **Back up your computer data.**
   Experienced computer users know that there are two types of people: those who have already lost data and those who are going to experience the pain of losing data in the future. Back up small amounts of data on floppy disks and larger amounts on CDs. If you have access to a network, you should save copies of your data on another computer on the network. Most people make weekly backups of all their important data. And make sure you have your original software start-up disks handy and available in the event your computer system files get damaged. Be prepared!

8. **Regularly download security protection update "*patches*."**
   Most major software companies today have to release updates and patches to their software every so often. Sometimes bugs are discovered in a program that may allow a malicious person to attack your computer. When these bugs are discovered, the software companies, or vendors, create patches that they post on their Web sites. You need to be sure you download and install the patches! Check your software vendors' Web sites on a regular basis for new security patches or use the new automated patching features that some companies offer. If you don't have the time to do the work yourself, download and install a utility program to do it for you. There are available software programs that can perform this task for you. Stay informed!

9. **Check your security on a regular basis. When you change your clocks for daylight saving time, reevaluate your computer security.**
   The programs and operating system on your computer have many valuable features that make your life easier, but can also leave you vulnerable to hackers and viruses. You should evaluate your computer security at least twice a year — do it when you change the clocks for daylight saving! Look at the settings on applications that you have on your computer. Your browser software, for example, typically has a security setting in its preferences area. Check what settings you have and make sure you have the security level appropriate for you. Set a high bar for yourself!

10. **Make sure your family members and/or your employees know what to do if your computer becomes infected.**
    It's important that everyone who uses a computer be aware of proper security practices. People should know how to update virus protection software, how to download security patches from software vendors, and how to create a proper password. Make sure they know these tips too!

APPENDIX F
THE *SYSTEMS ASSURANCE AND CONTROL (SAC) MODEL*

Audit Assurance

Audit assurance addresses information reliability. Auditors must look far beyond the presentation of information into the infrastructures supporting the creation, accumulation, processing, management, communication, and protection of information. The complexity of these infrastructures, their inner workings, and their interdependencies are enormous. Threats against the reliability and security of information, including the ethics of those controlling the information, exist across a broad array of technologies and processes and at varying levels of detail.

The array of risks potentially impacting information security defies identification. Logically then, one might ask: "What does an auditor's assurance of information reliability mean?" The answer must take into account the risks assessed, the basis for reliance on controls, the likelihood that significant problems exist that were not discovered, and/or the possibility of failure in one or more audit processes. Increasing recognition of both the importance and vulnerability of information and its supporting infrastructures is driving the auditing profession to seek new approaches and new models as the basis for assessing risks and providing assurance.

In the continuously changing business environment a standard may be obsolete before the community to which it applies can conclude whether it is too generic or too specific. But leading organizations that depend on their data and infrastructures understand the unacceptable costs of being unable to access information, provide services, or keep sensitive data private. Such organizations are keenly aware of the need for a structured control environment, and take the necessary steps to maintain such an environment.

The Institute of Internal Auditors and The IIA Research Foundation have, for many years, served the auditing profession by putting into practice the motto "Progress Through Sharing." The essential control and audit practices in well-run organizations are often studied, documented, and presented to the auditing profession at large in the form of standards, professional guidance, and practice aids. The *Systems Assurance and Control (SAC)* reports are one of the best and most enduring examples of progress through sharing in action.

The *SAC* Reports

For the auditing profession, knowledge of technology is a key differentiator between effectiveness and obsolescence. To that end, the *Systems Auditability and Control (SAC)* reports, originally published in 1977 by The Institute of Internal Auditors (IIA), with updates in 1991 and 1994 by The IIA Research Foundation, have consistently been recognized as landmark publications providing critical guidance and reference information in all areas where auditors must deal with technology and the related business issues.

Since the technology evolution has been dramatic in the past decade, *SAC* content is now being continuously updated to address e-business technologies and the myriad other issues that have emerged with widespread use of the Internet. *Systems Assurance and Control (SAC)* now brings executive management, corporate governance entities, and auditors new information to understand, monitor, assess, and mitigate technology risks. *SAC* examines and assesses risks that accompany each organizational component, including customers, competitors, regulators, community, and owners.

Further, the *SAC* reports provide a framework to guide an evaluation of business controls. The effective practices and control approaches of industry leaders, as viewed by their auditors, are the basis for the new *SAC* control and assessment model. To emphasize technology's business impacts and electronic delivery of the new material, electronic is added to the title. The title is further enhanced by changing "Auditability" to "Assurance," to recognize the important perspectives of governance and the alliances — both within an organization and between business partners — needed to assure effective security, auditability, and control of information.

The *SAC Model*

Internal auditors must understand the business risks resulting from changes in technology. They then must articulate responsive risk management strategies to management, and provide assurance on the availability, capability, functionality, protectability, accountability, and auditability of the systems, networks, and infrastructures involved. (Many auditors also interpret the traditional definition of information security — including confidentiality, integrity, and availability — as equivalent to the auditor's focus on information reliability.)

The *SAC Model* was developed to facilitate discussions of these issues. As COSO's (see www.coso.org) *Internal Control - Integrated Framework* provided a common control language for management and auditors, the *SAC Model* facilitates the discussion of objectives, risks, and mitigation responses within the context of e-business. Its purpose is to focus on how the risks resulting from rapid technology and e-business model changes can be managed, both in discussion and implementation.

The Sarbanes-Oxley legislation — which requires management reporting on the system of internal controls and external auditor attestation regarding management's assertions — also serves to heighten the emphasis on a reliable model for categorizing and assessing internal controls.

There are many different risk and control models, and each must be tailored to any given organization. Topics such as the rapidly evolving regulatory environment, how much capacity is enough, and making realistic technology choices are only a few of the significant issues that can be reviewed through the lens of the *SAC Model*.

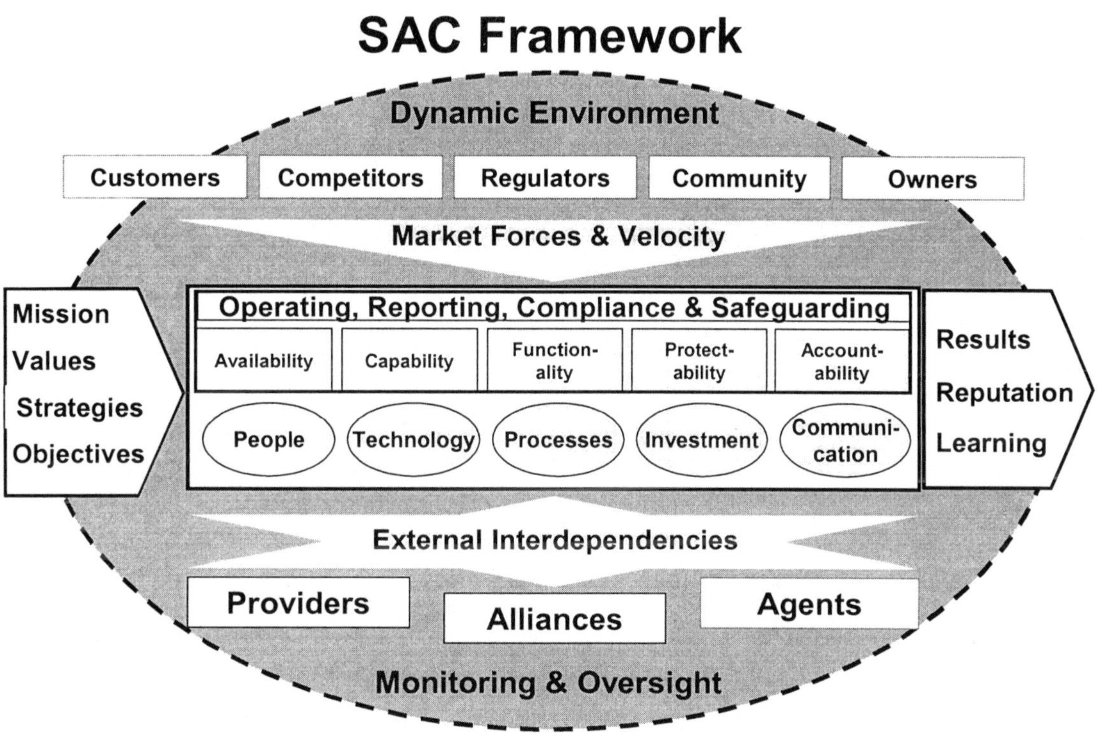

SAC Model Description

Since it has been successfully employed in numerous organizations, the COSO framework of objectives, risks, and controls (mitigating responses) has been employed as an integral part of the

SAC Model. From a global perspective, similar reports, such as Cadbury in the UK, have been issued worldwide and use the same general concepts, so this model should be easily adapted in any environment.

An organization typically pursues its mission (purpose) by establishing strategies and objectives consistent with its values. The arrow at the left side of the model indicates this process. The organization aims to achieve desired results while enhancing or preserving its reputational standing and learning how to improve its future performance. These outcomes are shown as the arrow at the right of the framework.

A sound control environment helps an organization stay on its intended path as it moves from mission to results. The broad control context — effectiveness and efficiency of operations, financial and other management reporting, compliance with laws and regulations, and safeguarding of assets (COSO objectives) — is captured in the top center of the framework. These are abbreviated for presentation as Operating, Reporting, Compliance, and Safeguarding.

Availability, Capability, Functionality, Protectability, and Accountability (in the next row) capture control attributes that are particularly pertinent for e-business activities. These can equally be called business assurance objectives, since they are broader than the way in which some people view control. These assurance objectives provide the "framework" through which *SAC* topics or modules are discussed. For instance, privacy concerns are addressed under Protectability and Accountability.

Availability

Information, processes, and services must be available when needed. Specifically, the organization must be able to receive, accept, process, and support transactions in a manner acceptable to its customers. For applications that are accessed via the Internet, 24/7 availability is often required. To ensure availability levels are acceptable, the auditor evaluates controls that deal with potential causes of business interruption. These might include:

- Physical and logical security of system resources.
- Mechanical failure of file storage devices, servers, etc.
- Malfunction of software or unexpected incompatibilities.
- Inadequate capacity planning.

In the event of a problem, controls must provide for swift recovery.

Capability

Capability means end-to-end reliability and timely completion and fulfillment of all transactions. This means systems must have adequate capacity, communications bandwidth, and other resources to consistently meet needs, even at peak demand. For systems to provide such services, monitoring of usage and service levels is critical, including services obtained from external sources, such as Internet service providers and application service providers. System and process bottlenecks must be identified and eliminated or carefully managed. The goal is to achieve and maintain an efficient and effective balance across the organization.

Efficiency of systems is an aspect of capability that should be monitored and optimized to ensure effective use of resources. System development and acquisition methodologies must be controlled to prevent cost overruns and systems that do not perform as required. To help ensure IT efficiency, the auditor evaluates controls that address the causes and risks of excessive costs, which can be characterized as waste and inefficiency. Typical problems might include:

- Weaknesses in controls that result in excessive correction of errors (prevention is usually more efficient).
- Controls that consume more resources than the benefits they deliver.

The objective is an optimal balance of control, which invariably includes the acceptance of some risk. Systems that are inefficient may foster user creation of shadow systems that work around the official system. Such duplicate costs are clearly inefficient. The unreliable system must be fixed before the shadow system is halted. The objective of system development controls is to avoid such issues. Methodologies should result in efficient and appropriate design and development of an application, and ensure that controls, auditability, and security are built into the system.

An information system that is not maintained effectively becomes unreliable. Controls over maintenance, often called change controls, provide continuity while hardware or software changes are made, and ensure that all changes are documented, approved, and confirmed. Maintenance controls cover issues such as adequate user involvement in requesting, testing, and approving program changes; creating appropriate audit trails, including program change history logs; IT and user personnel approval; and sufficient documentation of program changes. Production transfer controls are also important to reduce the risk of programmers having the ability to introduce unapproved test versions into production. (Change control is a complex issue, with many components to consider. These are indicated as examples only.)

Functionality

Functionality means the system provides the facilities, responsiveness, and ease-of-use to meet user needs. Good functionality goes well beyond minimum transaction processing. It should also provide control information and address other issues of concern to management. Preventing problems in functionality includes considering the perspective of untrained, possibly unknown, online users. Users can become impatient and may quit without completing a transaction or may resubmit input, causing duplicates. To help ensure functionality, the auditor evaluates controls that monitor and provide feedback. Some of these might include the display of progress indicators following input, positive confirmation of transactions, or monitoring user abandonment of transactions or "hang-ups."

Effective information is relevant to the business process delivered by a functional system. Relevance of information is based on system design, which requires user and management participation to ensure appropriate functionality. Problems often stem from inadequate specifications due to lack of user involvement in development, which usually means the resulting application will be ineffective.

To help ensure effectiveness, the auditor evaluates controls over timely, correct, consistent, and usable information. The format in which information is delivered can have a substantial impact on the effectiveness of communication, so displays and reports that can be tailored to different audiences can be a significant advantage.

Protectability

Protectability includes protection of hardware, software, and data from unauthorized access, use, or harm. Robust security is difficult to maintain for Internet-connected systems, since the structure of the Internet itself has inherent weaknesses. Controls are needed to safeguard IT assets against loss, and identify when such loss has occurred. Many current controls focus on reducing risks of catastrophic damage, internal fraud, or embezzlement. To ensure protectability, the auditor evaluates general controls over IT that are often grouped as follows:

- *Data Security and Confidentiality* — Data is an important asset, and access should be limited to those who are authorized to process or maintain specific data or records. Protecting organizational data is the key responsibility of the information security function and its administrator(s). Security functions may include restricting access to data through various logical access paths based on user requirements; restricting access to program libraries and data files on a "need-to-know" basis; and providing the ability to hold users accountable for activities performed.

- *Program Security* — Access to program files and libraries should be restricted to authorized personnel through use of access control and other security software. Program updates should be monitored and controlled using library management software. Appropriate segregation of duties should ensure that the programming function does not have unrestricted access to production programs.

- *Physical Security* — Access to processors and storage devices should be limited to those (e.g., management and operations staff) requiring access to perform job functions. Access to the host server computer room should be monitored and controlled (e.g., card access systems). Physical control over reports containing confidential data should be implemented (e.g., distribution procedures). Physical safeguards include fire prevention, preventive maintenance, backup of data files, and property insurance.

Many protectability objectives are designed to ensure data retains its integrity. In other words, data is complete, accurate, and up-to-date, and cannot be changed by unauthorized applications or users. To help ensure integrity, the auditor evaluates controls over the causes of erroneous data, often characterized as application controls, in addition to the general access controls described above. More detailed integrity controls may be needed to ensure the following objectives:

- Authorized transactions are initially and completely recorded.
- All transactions are completely and accurately entered into the system for processing.
- Approved transactions are accepted by the system when they are entered, and then processed to completion.
- All transactions are processed only once; no duplicate transactions are processed.
- All transactions are processed accurately, updating the correct files and records.

Procedures should minimize the opportunity for programmers and users to make unauthorized changes to production programs. Access to system software should be controlled to avoid direct compromises of the integrity of program code, data, and processing results.

Confidentiality and privacy are key issues not only for protectability, but also for controlling compliance and legal risk. As one expert said at one of The IIA's Critical Infrastructure Conferences: "Without security, there is no privacy." Confidentiality usually refers to intellectual property, trade secrets, competitive plans, or national security. Privacy is usually viewed in the context of personal information, including data associated with customers, employees, and stockholders, but not corporate entities. The Internet facilitates a new level of low-cost data collection. As a result, personal information has become an industry in itself. Organizations clearly need to maintain essential data about individuals to accomplish their missions, yet many currently go far beyond the minimum. The legal and regulatory environment is changing to address this, and it is critical to monitor these changes and audit business risk.

Accountability

Accountability identifies individual roles, actions, and responsibilities. It includes the concepts of data ownership, identification, and authentication, all of which are fundamental to being able to identify who or what caused a transaction. The auditor or transaction trail should have enough information — and be retained long enough — for transactions to be confirmed, if necessary.

Accountability includes the concept of non-repudiation. This means that, once authenticated, a user cannot disclaim a transaction, as might happen when an online brokerage user seeks to back out of a trade they initiated, simply because it turned out to be a bad idea.

Accountability also includes issues in granting traceable access to restricted information and software functions. This is a particular problem in IT, where systems analysts and administrators often resist the implementation of controls over their own activities. In some cases, monitoring can be turned off by the very individual it is designed to watch.

Organizations need to authenticate the identity of people entrusted with authority to change data files or software. Similarly, an organization holding private information has an obligation to authenticate the identity of inquirers before disclosing information. In such cases, accountability and privacy may appear to be in conflict, since accountability means identifying the source of a transaction, while privacy might deny meaningful identification. These objectives can be reconciled, but care is required. Accountability protects everyone, for example, when a seller has a legitimate need to authenticate the identity of a buyer for credit purposes, while the holder of the credit card has a legitimate need to authenticate the seller to prevent fraudulent misrepresentation.

To support accountability, information must be sufficient, accurate, timely, and available to management to meet its responsibilities. To help ensure reliability of information, the auditor evaluates controls over unacceptable processing and reporting. Capabilities might include each of the following.

- Information can be supported irrefutably. Controls that provide support are variously known as transaction trails or audit trails.
- Information should be timely. It must be available when decisions are made. This is a common criticism of financial statements issued months after the events.
- Information must be consistent and in accordance with applicable policies. Errors due to inappropriate processing, whether programmed or human, are common causes of inconsistent information. Management override can be another.

Achieving Assurance Objectives

Achieving Availability, Capability, Functionality, Protectability, and Accountability requires adequate infrastructure, resources, and organizational commitment. Necessary building blocks include: people, technology, processes, investment, and communication, which are shown in the ovals in the third band at the center of the *SAC* diagram.

This already complex environment has to effectively respond to external forces, which are depicted as multidirectional arrows in the diagram. The impact of ever-increasing interaction, interconnectivity, and system sharing with external entities (customers, competition, regulators, community, and owners); the increasing rate of change (velocity); and the quantity of external interdependencies (providers, alliances, and agents) are indications of just how many forces are affecting the e-business environment.

Dynamic Environment

The context to all of this is shown by the gray oval. The dynamic environment is often called the control environment, although many people today prefer to talk about risks and responses rather than controls. To enable stability and control, Monitoring and Oversight are key elements. Monitoring and oversight mean pertinent risks, whether internal or external to the organization, are recognized and addressed on an ongoing basis and controls are confirmed to be functioning as intended. These requirements are shown as the background, and must be effectively designed for all this to work.

Auditors are moving to other areas of monitoring, such as logging, and are testing to understand where deficiencies and problems may occur. In a world where electronic records are the order of the day and paper is truly disappearing, auditors can no longer expect to rely on familiar tangibles such as source documents. Today's source can be a Web-based input form, or an electronic transmission from another system. Pertinent questions include:

- What is the business objective? The goal of an e-business may not be clearly articulated, and those depending on it may require after-the-fact definitions and strategies.
- What are the risks? Technology platforms are non-homogenous and interlinked, often with outside agents. How can network security in a network of networks be assessed (the Internet and those of business allies)?
- Where are the controls? Traditional views may be inadequate, since there is a need to look to the infrastructure, business processes, and middleware glue that hold it all together (whereas formerly one simply reviewed general controls and application controls).

As an example of the *SAC Model* in action, the following "heat map" shows how the framework can be used to report the status of controls. Since the ovals in the third central band are control building blocks, the heat map illustrates how the model might be used to drill down to root cause issues, discussing each according to its priority and potential consequences.

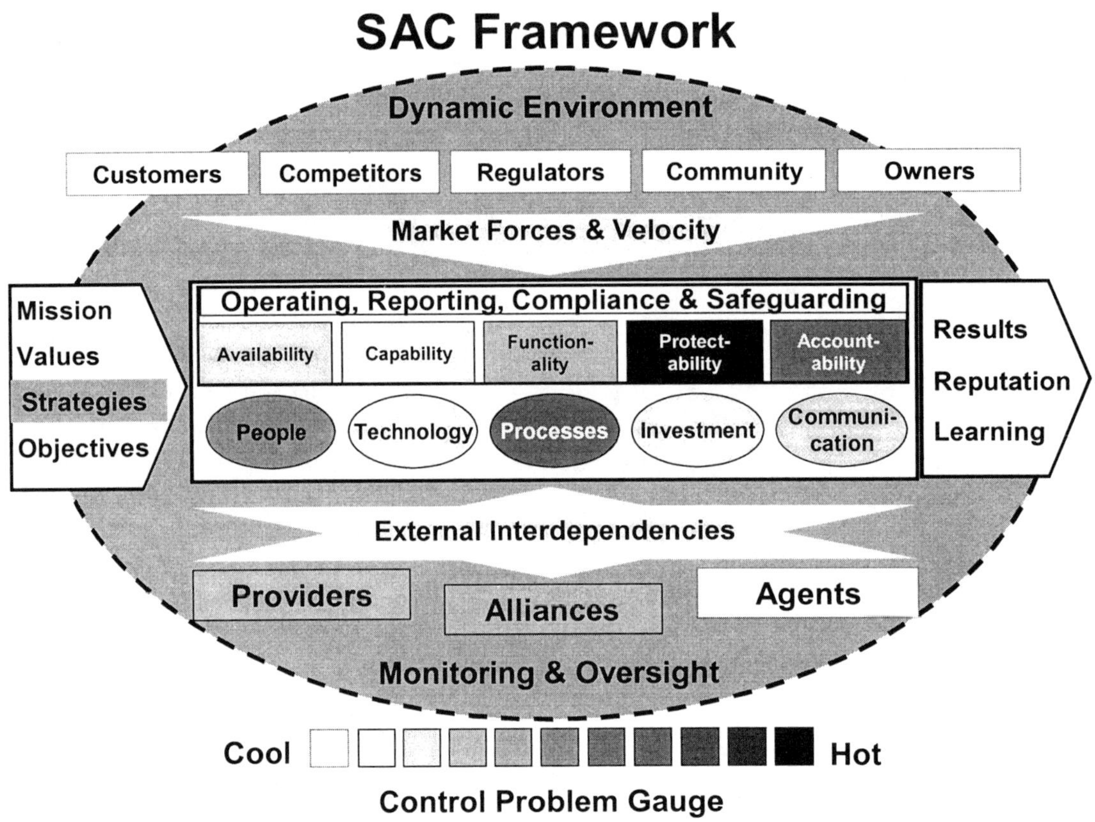

Summary

Availability, Capability, Functionality, Protectability, and Accountability are business assurance objectives. What they mean in this context is:

- Availability — Able to receive, accept, process, and support transactions at all times, as required (e.g., 24/7).
- Capability — There is end-to-end reliable, timely completion and fulfillment of all transactions.
- Functionality — Systems provide necessary facilities, responsiveness, and ease-of-use to meet user needs and expectations.
- Protectability — Logical and physical security controls ensure authorized access, and deny unauthorized access, to servers, applications, and information assets.
- Accountability — Transaction processing is accurate, complete, and non-refutable (non-repudiation).

Relating Control Objectives to the *SAC Model*

There is a variety of depth and coverage in statements regarding control objectives. For example, integrity is a top-level control criterion in CobiT, and an inherent requirement in the COSO report on reliability of financial reporting. The level of detail varies, with CobiT's four domains, seven information criteria, 34 high-level control objectives, and 318 detailed control objectives, to address specific issues and control concerns.

Based on those widely used sources, the components of major pronouncements as they apply to the *SAC Model* are shown in the table on the following page:

Control Objectives and Consequences					
SAC Model	**COSO**	**SysTrust**	**CobiT Information criteria**	**Objectives — consensus**	**Consequences**
Availability		Available	Available	Reliable Available	Business interruption Loss of customers
Capability	Reporting Efficient	Integrity	Integrity Efficient	Effective	Erroneous record keeping Excessive costs/ deficient revenues
Functionality	Effective	Maintainability	Effective	Capability Efficient Functionality	Erroneous management decisions Fails user & business needs Fails user & business needs
Protectability	Safeguarding	Security	Confidential	Compliance Accountability	Loss or destruction of assets Fraud
Accountability	Reliable Compliance		Reliable Compliance	Integrity Maintainability Confidential Security	Unacceptable accounting Statutory sanctions Competitive disadvantage Deniable/ anonymous actions

Training Objectives for Auditors in E-business

- Understand key information technology risk components and ways to mitigate those risks.
- Develop knowledge of information systems auditing and assurance services terms and procedures, including an awareness of advanced auditing and information processing concepts.
- Identify sources for research of technology risk.
- Utilize the Internet as a research and communication tool for information technology risk management and auditing.
- Learn the controls and key questions to ask concerning controls from an end-user standpoint, to enable effective auditing of end-user training and processes.
- Learn the key components of a well-controlled data processing department. Also, be able to explain why these controls are necessary. If there are compensating controls, be able to explain why certain controls may not be necessary.
- Be able to adapt an audit checklist and audit program to various information systems environments.
- Develop skills necessary to perform an information systems audit and prepare an audit report.
- Be able to describe the common features of audit software and the situations in which they would best be used.
- Develop an in-depth understanding of risk management topics as they relate to specific, relevant information systems.
- Develop the knowledge required to sit for and pass the Certified Internal Auditor (CIA), and the Certified Information Systems Auditor (CISA) examinations.
- Learn to monitor those areas of technology risk that are of greatest concern, as identified by The IIA, AICPA, ISACA, SANS, CIS, and other leaders in auditing and information security.
- Identify and evaluate risks in an e-business environment.
- Understand how to adapt audit coverage in areas of advanced and emerging technologies.
- Learn to recognize opportunities where improvements in control techniques and audit practices, such as intelligent monitors and audit analytics, can significantly improve an organization's ability to protect against threats, mitigate risks, and recover from disruptions or destruction.

Credits

Most of the material in this appendix is taken directly from the *SAC Model* module of The IIA Research Foundation's *Systems Assurance and Control* reports. *SAC* represents professional guidance from The IIA. *SAC* can be accessed using the "Technology" button on The IIA's Web site at www.TheIIA.org. Additional information is also available via The IIA's ITAudit.org Web site, also accessible via the "Technology" button on TheIIA.org.

The assurance section at the beginning of this document is consistent with other guidance from The IIA, but is not taken directly from *SAC*. Most of the content in the Training Objectives section was provided by Mark Salamasick from the syllabus of the course he teaches at the University of Texas in Dallas.

APPENDIX G
ENTERPRISE PC MANAGEMENT AUDIT ASSESSMENT

The following assessment guide is a summary of the contents throughout this report of the key areas that should be reviewed and assessed by management. It is consistent with the COSO model presented in the report, the survey performed as part of the research, and the Sarbanes-Oxley Act, and follows The IIA's *International Standards for the Professional Practice of Internal Auditing (Standards)*. It is not, however, meant to be a substitute for discussion around detail issues; it is meant to be a guide for auditors and management.

For ease of understanding, and for international applicability, the guide is organized using the newly drafted Enterprise Risk Management Conceptual Framework, which expanded the original COSO model. At the time of this publication the new framework was not finalized and was out for review. The items below can also be used as a starting point for discussion on the internal audit of the networked PC infrastructure. For more detailed best practices on PC security, see Appendix E with tips from CERT and the National Cyber Security Alliance.

Environment

- Determine "tone from the top on control environment related to PC network infrastructure" from corporate directors, management, technology, and users for awareness to overall networked PC issues in the enterprise.
- Determine if groups such as finance, legal, risk management, purchasing, security, technology, and audit have an integrated view of the networked PC environment. This should include working as a collaborative group to address the total cost of ownership and security issues.
- Review corporate policies and procedures for PC security, and determine appropriateness and adequacy.
- Determine adequacy of asset management practices throughout the corporate enterprise for the PC.
- Determine status of overall management processes and documentation for networked PC infrastructure components.
- Determine processes in place for inclusion of new technologies such as wireless and personal digital assistants (PDA) for introduction and integration into overall corporate policies and practices.

- Determine how effectively management practices address timing and business requirements for the introduction of emerging technologies into the overall technology infrastructure.
- Review and determine adequacy of corporate standards, management, and governance groups related to PC processes.

Event Identification

- Determine which events impact the networked PC environment within the enterprise. Include events such as power outages, virus attacks, errors in software updates, hacker intrusions, and risk to the business units.
- Determine plans for dealing with PC operating system and application software that is no longer supported by the vendor.
- Determine technologies that have significant positive or negative impact on the enterprise and the strategy in dealing with the new technology (i.e., PDAs, wireless PC).

Risk Assessment

- Determine if PCs are included in overall corporate risk assessment processes, including business resumption and insurance.
- Review processes in place to survey and determine risk for individual PC environments. Determine if high business risk areas justify a different level of controls.
- Determine if a gap analysis has been performed for insurance coverage to address various security issues resulting from the PC such as software patch management, cyber incidents, and failure to comply with regulatory statutes.
- Review how internal audit is addressing the networked PC as part of the internal audit process.

Risk Response

- Determine type of response to deal with gaps in controls for the PC infrastructure.
- Determine if response is adequate or if additional mitigating controls or insurance coverage should be provided.
- Determine if the balancing of risk/cost is adequate to deal with the complex enterprise PC environment.

Control Activities

- Determine appropriateness and adequacy of processes in place to provide for backup and recovery of individual PC user data and operating system environment. Select a sample and test for compliance with standards.
- Determine and evaluate processes in place for software patch management. Review company standard to vendor specifications. Review processes for effectiveness and efficiency. Select a sample and test for adherence to vendor required standards or perform system scan of all PCs out of compliance.
- Review procedures for providing individual updates of virus definitions. Review and compare company standard for virus definitions to those of the vendor. Determine adequacy of distribution processes for virus updates. Select a sample and test adherence to standards or perform system scan of all PCs to determine amount of out of compliance PCs.
- Determine if adequate standards are established for a minimum number of standard desktop and notebook configurations.
- Review procedures for PC life cycle management and migration. Determine adequacy of the defined process and standardization of refresh cycle. Select a sample to test adherence to standards or perform a system scan of all PCs to determine degree of equipment out of compliance hardware.
- Determine if practices related to disposal of older PCs is appropriate. Review the sample from the previous step and determine if enhancements to enforcement of disposal of PCs are required.
- Review the process for determining the PC total cost of ownership. Compare the model to standards and ensure all components such as virus protection, support costs, and PC disposal are included in the model. Verify accuracy of metrics in model and compare to market best practices.
- Review corporate policies and practices for prohibited software on PCs. Select a sample of PCs or perform a search of all PCs for prohibited software. Determine appropriate action.
- If end users are not allowed to have system administrator capabilities on the PCs determine level of compliance with this policy. Select a sample of PCs or perform scan of all PCs to determine compliance with this policy.
- If users are provided administrator access to PCs, determine the adequacy of alternative controls to contain the potential negative impacts of such access.
- If encryption of data is performed from the PC through the network, select a sample and perform appropriate tests to determine compliance.
- If compliance of corporate policies related to the networked PC is an issue, review automated controls to ensure compliance with these practices. Determine if recommendation for automating processes with PC would be appropriate.

**Note: For sampling in this section, include both notebook and desktop computers in the sample since the processes for these may be significantly different. Consider scanning all PC systems if tools are in place to perform this testing. If these software management tools are not in place, discuss with network and security management the opportunity to utilize an automated solution for assessing compliance with corporate policies and practices.

Information & Communication

- Determine the level of corporate communication related to PC security policy and procedures. Determine if all corporate communication channels are used to the extent necessary (intranet, e-mail, newsletters, broadcast messages, and staff meetings).
- Review scripts from the PC help desk to assess the adequacy of continual education on PC practices and security issues.
- Assess the training provided to PC help desk employees on security and control issues. Determine the effectiveness of these training programs and the integration of security issues into help desk functions.
- Determine if PC user surveys are used in the enterprise. Review results from the surveys and determine if enhancements should be made for security/control issues.
- Review reports for help desk calls related to security, virus, and control issues. Determine if any patterns exist and if additional training or modification of procedures is required.

Monitoring

- Determine what reports management uses to review and manage the PC environment.
- Determine how monthly PC help desk reports are used, and assess the level of corporate communication related to PC security policy and procedures. Determine if all corporate communication channels are used to the extent necessary (intranet, e-mail, newsletters, broadcast messages, and staff meetings).
- Determine what reports management uses for measuring the total cost of ownership of the PC environment. Determine if adequate metrics and monitoring are in place to drive down the long-term cost per unit.
- For high-risk business areas, determine what assessment management and audits are performed for PC-related functions.
- Determine if regular security scanning is employed to monitor virus protection, software patch updates, and the use of unauthorized software and security exposures.
- Determine if an assessment of the insurance for networked PCs has been performed.
- Determine if a gap analysis has been performed for risks not covered in the general liability policy to assess the need for additional coverage.

IIA Research Foundation Board of Trustees

IIA Research Foundation
Board of Research Advisors

IIA RESEARCH FOUNDATION

Chairman's Circle

ABN AMRO North America, Inc.
Cargill, Inc.
ChevronTexaco Corporation
Entergy Services, Inc.
Ernst & Young LLP
ExxonMobil Corporation
General Motors Corporation
Intel Corporation
Microsoft Corporation
PricewaterhouseCoopers LLP

THE INSTITUTE OF INTERNAL AUDITORS
International Advanced Technology Committee

Chairman
Jay Stott, CIA, *Fidelity Investments*

Vice Chairman
Christian Hendricks, CIA, *U.S. House of Representatives*

Members
Frank Alvern, CIA, CCSA, *Nordea*
Alexandre Alves Apparecido, *Brasil Telecom*
Ken D. Askelson, CIA, *JCPenney Company Inc.*
Dror Aviv, CFSA, *IIA Israel*
Donald L. Bailey, *Grant Thornton, LLP*
E.W. Sean Ballington, *PricewaterhouseCoopers, LLP*
Norman F. Barber, *Protiviti Inc.*
Juan De Dios Bel, *Instituto de Auditores Internos de Argentina*
David F. Bentley, *Consultant*
Marc Chambault, *France Telecom*
Michael P. Fabrizius, CIA, *Bon Secours Health System Inc.*
Ramiz Tofigi Ganizade, *Azerbaijan Republic Chamber of Auditors*
Miguel Gneco, CIA, *Deloitte & Touche*
Douglas Guerrero, *EDS Corporation*
Jose Manuel Gutierrez Juvera, *Best Decision SC*
Ulrich Hahn, CIA, *Syngenta International*
David J. Hill, *IBM Corporation*
Michael S. Hines, CIA, *Purdue University*
Mark J. Hornung, *Ernst & Young LLP*
Gene Kim, *Tripwire Inc.*
Walter G. Kozikowski, *Mayo Clinic*
Gerard Lepine, *Societe Immobiliere Du Quebec*
David S. Lione, *KPMG LLP Southeast Region*
Steve Mar, *Microsoft Corporation*
Denys Lucien Martin, CIA, *Laval University*
Peter B. Millar, *ACL Services Ltd.*
Allan M. Newstadt, CIA, *World Bank/IFC*
Brenda J. S. Putman, CIA, *City Utilities of Springfield*
Kyoko Shimizu, CIA, *Shin Nihon & Co.*
Brian M. Spindel, CIA, *SecurePipe Incorporated*
Jay R. Taylor, CIA, *General Motors Corporation*
Thomas Jason Wood, CIA, *Eastman Kodak Company*
Akitomo Yamamoto, *IIA Japan*

IIA Staff Liaison
Charles H. Le Grand, CIA, *Assistant Vice President, Technology Practices*